Ross A. Mueller

Table of Contents

Acknowledgments

A special thanks to my wife, Lois, a medical professional who is independent enough to allow my independence for my days on the stream.

To my son, Nate, for sacrificing valuable fishing time to help with streamside photographs.

To my daughter, Lisa, for providing lodging on my trips to Minnesota.

To the staff at Palmer Publications, Inc./Amherst Press, including Chuck Spanbauer, Christine Doyle, Heidi Bittner-Zastrow and Susan Scholten.

To my fishing companions who keep me well-apprised of hatches and conditions: Norm Zimmerman, Dick Ward, John Shillinglaw and Fred Corsmeier.

To Dick Pobst and Carl Richards for helpful advice, to George Close and Wayne Anderson for help with patterns and streamside expertise, and to Tom Andersen of Hudson, Wisconsin, for assistance and encouragement.

To Gary Borger for his gifts of time and wisdom.

To Dana Zimmerman for assistance and consultation with the manuscript.

To Murray Photo and Video, Appleton, Wisconsin, for use of photographic facilities.

And to all the fly fishers—too numerous to name—who taught me something.

INTRODUCTION

One of the great satisfactions of fly-fishing is discovering flies that work; another is communicating your discoveries and experiences to others. I'd like to communicate my experience regarding flies that work—how to tie and how to fish them.

When you've been captivated by fly-fishing as I have for the past 40 years, you learn a lot. Realizing that you need to develop a sensible collection of fly patterns does not take long, and you need to learn how and when to present the imitations to the trout. The process of developing a collection and learning the essentials of presentation is an educational evolution. This book is the result of my evolution and is intended to help fly fishers who want to learn more or who want to compare their experiences with mine.

What I've attempted to do is provide a collection of fly patterns that will see the fly fisher through most of the streamside situations likely to be encountered throughout the year. Because most of my day-to-day fishing is done in the upper Midwest (particularly Wisconsin), the collection represents Iowa, Minnesota, Michigan and Wisconsin.

TYING NOTES will explain how to construct the pattern at the desk. FISHING NOTES will explain how to use the pattern on the stream—the fun part! My particular favorite flies are marked with a ★. These patterns are selected for many reasons—not only for their effectiveness but for how I feel when I fish them. Leeches and scuds are nearly always effective, but when I see the first Blue-Winged Olives of the season with rising trout, I have a very good feeling for my Blue-Winged Olive Parachute. The same is true for Tricos or Hoppers.

My most important source of information has been my streamside notes, which I've kept for over 20 years. The notes detail year-round information such as hatch activity, pumped stomach contents, water conditions, etc. Each year the notes are summarized month by month, stream by stream, and the information is used to build a more meaningful base of knowledge. The notebooks also contain advice from experienced fly fishers and insights into the solutions of streamside problems. Other sources of information include my fly-fishing library, including many books that are noted in the list of references. Pertinent fly-fishing articles from magazines over the past 20 years have also been used.

The collection of patterns has been divided into two main groups: YEAR-ROUND and SEASONAL. The YEAR-ROUND flies should be carried throughout the year. Minnows, leeches, nymphs, scuds, etc. are present at all times in streams. Additionally, you're apt to encounter Midge hatches at any time and I've seen Blue-Winged Olives from February through December. I carry the larger streamer, leech, nymph, etc. patterns in a sheepskin wallet—smaller nymph, larva and scud patterns go in a swing-leaf fly box. Patterns classified as SEASONAL imply a certain period of emergence e.g. sulphurs in May-June, Tricos in July-August-September. The SEASONAL patterns are carried in appropriate fly boxes only during the periods of emergence that are given in the text and the Hatch Chart (page 94).

Needless to say, you'll be carrying more flies in summer than in winter. My intent with SEASONAL patterns is to include the hatches that will most likely be encountered and keep to an effective minimum the patterns for each hatch.

I had the good fortune to fish with the noted British fly fisherman, John Goddard, in New Zealand and was amazed at the small number of flies he carried. This experience was a stimulus to me to reduce the number of flies I carried. My fly collection, at the time, was the product of undisciplined tying and random buying.

You could probably get through the season with scud patterns sub-surface and Adams patterns on top, but it is more fun to tie and fish a good variety of patterns. The trout need variety as well, especially in catch and release areas, where they become conditioned to certain patterns and presentations.

Along with a map of streams mentioned, photographs and sketches of each pattern are included (pattern illustrations are not to scale). A list of reference material is provided. Because this book is more concerned with imitations than naturals, the references concerning identification of the naturals are of particular importance.

GETTING STARTED

This book presumes a basic familiarity with fly tying and stream fishing. Those unfamiliar with fly-fishing should be aware of the infinity of knowledge to be gained (even the experts admit they have a lot to learn). For the beginner, I would like to say that many excellent resources are available and would like to comment briefly about some foundations of fly-fishing skill.

Most importantly, fish with and talk with experienced fly fishers. Joining a Trout Unlimited or Federation of Fly Fishers chapter in your area is a good way to meet experts. Also, contact the people in your local trout shop; you will find them helpful. I still hire guides because they always teach me something of value. Take a fly tying course. I can't imagine fly-fishing without fly tying; tying your own flies will make you a better fly fisher. Fly casting is a critical skill; learning the basic casting stroke is not complicated. I've found several of the videotapes helpful (page 98). You will find that developing your casting skills is as much fun as the fishing—just like fly tying. Keep a streamside notebook. It will be a valuable guide at your fly tying desk.

Reading the water, understanding some of the entomology and expanding your repertoire of streams are all part of the infinity of knowledge. Because fly-fishing has become very popular, we all need to become familiar with issues such as habitat preservation and catch and release fishing.

This book will be helpful with your decisions of fly selection and presentation. Hopefully, it will lead you to advance your knowledge in other areas as well. You will find that the more you learn, the more there is to learn—a true lifetime experience.

NOTES ON TYING

Many of the patterns in this book are generated from streamside notes. The streamside naturals and pumped stomach specimens are sketched in actual size, and colors are noted using the Borger Color System (BCS)®. Carry one BCS tablet in your vest with your notebook, and keep one at your fly tying desk.

Hooks are a matter of personal preference—each of the separate brands has models that are reasonably equivalent. As an example, for nymph hooks, the MUSTAD® 9671, TIEMCO® (TMC) 3761, DAI-RIKI® 730 and DAIICHI® 1710 are similar. Before tying, crimp down the hook barbs. Barbless is as effective as barbed, and it's much easier to remove the hook from whatever you may catch: fish, moss or yourself. Also, removal of a barbless hook is easier on the fly.

Weighting the hook is noted in the text as light, medium and heavy. (See Figure 1.) Use lead or copper wire approximately the diameter of the hook wire, and wrap as drawn. Heavily weighted flies will drift upside down.

Figure 1: Weighting

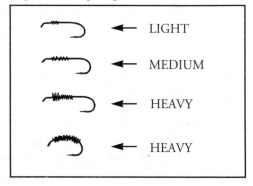

My most commonly used thread is Uni-Thread® size 6-0 and 8-0. For a vise, I mainly use a Renzetti® rotary or a Regal®. Each has its advantages. The rotary vise is unexcelled for winding hackle, dubbing and ribbing material. It positions the fly easily. The Regal® allows very rapid insertion/removal of the hook and has an unexcelled grip that is very useful when weighting a number of hooks. It also positions the fly well during tying.

Fly tying materials, of course, are critical—the following are some of my most-used materials:

Furs:

I think beaver is the best choice for small dries and nymphs. Beaver allows exact body tapers and is easy to dub. Natural gray, olive, brown and light yellow are my color preferences. Muskrat and mole are also very good. Australian opossum and hare's ear, picked-out, are excellent body materials on a wide range of flies. Snowshoe hare's foot fibers make excellent emerger wings.

Hairs:

I am always looking for good deer and elk hair for winging Compara-duns, caddis, etc. White calf body hair is useful as a divided up-wing, down-wing or parachute post. Moose fibers are excellent for tailing larger flies.

Feathers:

Peacock, marabou, pheasant tail, wood duck flank, CDC, biots, turkey of all sorts, soft hackles, quality rooster necks, saddles and duck quills are a good start to the list of essential feathers.

Synthetics:

My most-used synthetics include Krystal Flash®, Z-Lon®, Antron® and Synthetic Living Fiber® (SLF). SLF, in its varying degrees of coarseness, is excellent in many applications, especially with a dubbing loop. Twinkle organza is good as a spinner wing material or as a wing "additive."

Eyes:

Eyes are an important feature on larger flies—glass beads, brass beads, bead chain, lead, small jewelry spacers (dumbbell-shaped springs) and painted eyes are all useful.

My favorite "how-to" tying book is A. K. Best's *Production Fly Tying*. The books by Randall Kaufmann and Skip Morris listed in the reference section are also excellent (page 96).

Figure 2:

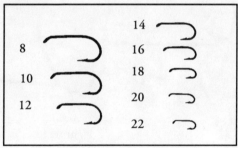

Actual Hook Sizes (Dry Fly Hooks)

Locator Map:
Streams mentioned in text

Wisconsin
1. Brule River
2. White River
3. Namekagon River
4. Oconto, South Branch Oconto River
5. Willow River
6. Kinnickinnic River
7. Wolf River
8. Tomorrow/Waupaca River
9. Timber Coulee
10. West Fork, Kickapoo River
11. Big and Little Green River
12. Castle Rock
13. Pine River
14. Willow River
15. White River
16. Mecan River
17. Black Earth Creek

Iowa
1. Bloody Run
2. Spring Branch

Michigan
1. Ontonagon River
2. Escanaba River
3. Pigeon River
4. Au Sable River
5. Pere Marquette River
6. Muskegon River

Minnesota
1. Whitewater River
2. Root River, South Branch Root River

CLASSIFICATION OF PATTERNS

YEAR-ROUND FLIES

As mentioned, YEAR-ROUND flies are carried throughout the year. These flies represent food items that are available to trout throughout most or all of the season.

Deep and Mid-Depth Flies

Gray Leech ★

Hook: Mustad® 9672—size 6,14

Weight: Heavy—concentrate weight toward front half of hook

Thread: Black 6-0

Head: Black glass bead, size 8-0

Tail: Natural gray turkey marabou—also excellent in black; as an option, a few strands of Mylar® Tinsel may be added to tail

Body: Same marabou as tail

Tying Notes: This fly is a very fast fly to tie. I view it as a "disposable" fly—it is often fished on the bottom and is prone to loss. To tie: pre-load glass beads (from fly shop or craft store) and weight a dozen hooks. The lead is wrapped in the thorax area and doubled back on itself to create a jig-like effect (see Figure 1) when fished. Tie in tail; then use thread to wrap, rib-like over the forward extension of the tail to create a thin abdomen. Dub marabou on the thread and create an enlarged thorax and tie-off. Brush back the thorax and abdomen with Velcro®. The Gray Leech is a variation of the All Marabou Leech, designed by Tom Wendelburg of Middleton, Wisconsin.

Fishing Notes:

Leeches in our midwestern streams are often dark gray, a color well matched by the gray marabou from a wild turkey.

The Gray Leech is an excellent wintertime fly. Fish the size 6 version by letting it settle to the bottom of pools, waiting for a minute or two, then very slowly retrieving along the bottom. In winter, don't look for trout in shallow undercuts; they are concentrated in deep, quiet water and are quite sluggish. Fishing the leech is most effective late in the afternoon after the water has reached its warmest temperature of the day. This is also the time the sun leaves the water, a situation that seems to activate larger trout. The brown trout pictured on the front cover was caught and released in February during the time of Wisconsin's early season. This fish and two others of similar size took a Gray Leech late in the afternoon after shadows covered the stream.

In warmer conditions, the fly can be fished in a variety of ways—upstream like a nymph or down and across like a streamer. It is a good fly to use when you need to get deep in a hurry, particularly when fishing man-made "lunker" structures. Here, the "deep dapping" technique can be deadly. Quietly approach over the underlying structure (see Figure 6) and drop the fly over the edge, keeping the rod tip minimally exposed. The quick-sinking fly will drop into view of the trout beneath you, and you can often see the flash of the fish as it exits its hide to take the fly.

The smaller version (size 14) is fished in the same way and is good for small streams and light fly rods.

The leech tied with black marabou is an excellent pattern in discolored water—it is surprisingly visible even in high, dirty water. Olive and white are also good colors.

Wooly Bugger

Hook: Mustad® 9672—size 4, 10

Weight: Medium

Thread: Black 6-0

Tail: Red marabou

Body: Black chenille

Hackle: Soft grizzly—palmered over body

Tying Notes: Leave a tag-end of tying thread after securing marabou tail and chenille. Wrap chenille forward, tie in hackle at front and wrap to rear; then secure hackle by winding the tag end of thread forward. The Wooly Bugger is tied in a multitude of colors and sizes. My crayfish imitation utilizes a brown or tan marabou tail and body with soft orange hackle tied in front and not palmered back. It is heavily weighted.

Fishing Notes:

This fly is a classic and, like the leech, may be fished in many ways. The red-tailed version is an excellent fly for high cloudy water—add a split shot at the nose and fish it upstream, casting close to either bank and twitching on the retrieve to allow the action of the marabou and soft hackle to pulsate as the fly is carried down-current.

Wooly Buggers are an excellent choice for large, deep pools, as in Minnesota's Whitewater system and Iowa's Bloody Run. Fish this fly at the drop-offs, edges and on the bottom.

Crayfish, or parts of crayfish, are common contents of trout stomachs. Trout seem to take crayfish at night or in the early morning hours. If you're seeing many crayfish fleeing ahead of you while you are wading rocky streams, consider using the imitation fished near the bottom. Use undulating movements to mimic the behavior of the natural.

Minnow Imitations (streamers)

There are some general conditions in which I favor a streamer—one is very early in the morning during the summer, around dawn, when the large, nocturnal feeding brown trout are still out and about, before the sun hits the water and before other anglers become active. Also, during mid-day lulls a streamer may be used to "invade the territory" of a good fish, resulting in a "territorial strike" rather than a "feeding strike." Sometimes after fishing upstream a few hours, when it's time to turn back, I'll tie on a streamer and fish it on the way down, casting to within inches of the opposite bank and twitch retrieving—casting practice. During the fall spawning time, where regulations permit, large streamers are very effective for the brown and brook trout, particularly on Great Lakes tributary streams. It is a good idea to tie a few very large streamers (or Wooly Buggers) of your own design for use under special conditions, particularly at night in an area where you may have located a very large fish.

The Clouser Deep Minnow, Muddler Minnow—Variant and Black Ghost are three effective streamer patterns presented.

Clouser Deep Minnow

Hook: Mustad® 9672—size 6, 8

Weight: Dumbbell lead eyes

Thread: Black 3-0 or 6-0

Body: Flat silver tinsel

Underbody: White marabou or bucktail

Overbody: Blue and green Krystal Flash® under optional brown and white bucktail

Tying Notes: Lash dumbbell eye to top of hook about one-third shank length behind eye and secure with Permabond® 102. Wrap body and tie short white marabou or bucktail on top just behind eye. Reverse hook in vise and add Krystal Flash and overlying bucktail, each in front of eye. Form a thread head. This should be a sparse tie.

Fishing Notes:

This is an upside-down fly that gets deep and rides hook up, resulting in fewer snags. It is good for deep runs with rocky bottoms, found in large rivers like Wisconsin's lower Oconto, Minnesota's Root and the Ontonagon system of Michigan's Upper Peninsula. Cast up and across current, mend upstream to allow the fly to sink, and allow it to drift through the run, letting it swing at the end of the drift, twitching on the retrieve. The Clouser Deep Minnow is an intelligent choice for deep "powerful" water at any time.

Muddler Minnow—Variant

Hook: Mustad® 9672—size 6, 10

Weight: Tier's preference—I prefer medium

Thread: Black 6-0

Tail: Gray squirrel tail with black and white tip exposed—may substitute marabou

Body: Flat gold tinsel

Underwing: Gray squirrel tail or marabou

Overwing: A bit of untrimmed deer hair from head

Head: Spun deer hair, clipped to bullet-shape

Tying Notes: The muddler is another classic, and tying instructions abound. Black, white or yellow are good colors for the marabou muddler.

Fishing Notes:

This is a good fly to use anywhere, from small spring creeks to large freestone rivers. I prefer casting the muddler across and slightly downstream, casting as close to the opposite bank as possible—within inches. Let the fly swing and add motion by twitching the rod tip or stripping in line. Usually fished mid-depth, the fly is visible and you can see the take. At times, a large trout will "chase the minnow" out of its territory but not take it—you've just located a good fish to return to later.

Huge trout, especially browns, become a different "species" as compared to their smaller kin when it comes to feeding habits. They go on brief feeding binges, often under the cover of darkness or in discolored water, devouring large prey items such as minnows and crayfish. Following the feeding period, they rest in sheltered areas and are difficult to catch. The Muddler Minnow and Wooly Bugger (page 12) are good choices for fishing when large trout are vulnerable. The fly should make a commotion in the water, a hard splash on entry, combined with an active retrieve—hopefully, a larger commotion will follow!

Black Ghost

Hook: TMC® 300—size 12

Weight: None

Thread: Black 6-0

Tail: Short tuft yellow marabou

Body: Black floss

Rib: Optional flat medium silver tinsel

Wing: 4 white hackle feathers

Throat: Short sparse yellow marabou

Head: Black thread with painted eye—white with black pupil

Tying Notes: See A. K. Best's book, Production Fly Tying, *for tying in wing and painting eye. I use Testors® enamel from a hobby store and coat with head cement when dry. Eyes are an important feature on larger imitations.*

Fishing Notes:

Guided by Herb Weigl, of Cold Spring Anglers in Carlisle, Pennsylvania, this fly produced a 27-inch brown trout, not in the Midwest, but on Pennsylvania's Le Tort (see photo, Colorplate 4). Needless to say, it got my attention. Herb recommended standing on or close to the bank and casting the fly down-current, at an angle of about 45 degrees. Mend upstream and feed out line to let the fly slowly swing to the bank below you; then slowly strip-retrieve upstream towards you—add a split shot at the nose if needed. This old wet fly technique has proven deadly on medium to small heavily fished streams. It is used to explore "trouty"-looking banks downstream and on the same side from which you are casting. (See Figure 3.)

Figure 3:

Fishing "trouty" water down-current, same side of bank. The fly is cast about 45 degrees down-current, upstream mends are made to keep the head of the fly up-current and line is fed out to enable the fly to drift beneath the overhanging obstruction. The fly is swung near the bank and twitch retrieved. If no mending is done and no line fed out, the fly will end up at position A.

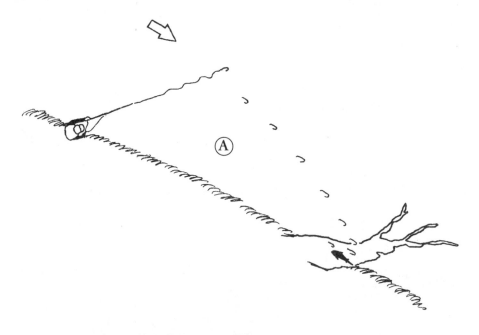

This brown trout took a Caddis Larva at the drop off of a riffle.

San Juan Worm

Hook: Mustad® 9672 or Dai-Riki® 710-C—size 12

Weight: None

Thread: Orange 6-0

Head: Optional red or pearl glass bead

Body. Ultra-Chenille® in red, claret, gray and "earthworm"

Tying Notes: Super easy—simply lash the chenille to the hook and burn the tips to taper. About half my worms have one or more glass beads, at the head, which add just the right amount of weight for small water.

Fishing Notes:

Trout like to eat worms. As has been said in another context by Brian Clarke and John Goddard, authors of one of my all-time favorite trout books *The Trout and the Fly*, "Why deny them the pleasure?" Fish the worm like a nymph by casting upstream, using a split-shot about six inches above the fly and an indicator. The worm is also good as the upper fly of a two-fly system. (See Figure 10.) It is at its best during or after a rain on all streams.

Girdle Bug

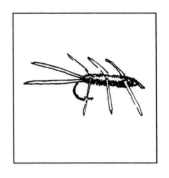

Hook: Mustad® 9672—size 10, 14

Thread: Black 6-0

Weight: Medium to light

Body: Black or olive chenille—can use crystal chenille

Tail and Legs: White rubber legs

Tying Notes: This is another easy fly to tie. Tie in a strand of rubber legs material and double it back for a "two-pronged" tail. Tie in chenille and advance thread toward eye, tying in two or three sets of rubber legs as you progress forward. Wind chenille forward and tie off.

Fishing Notes:

The Girdle Bug is at its best as a mid-depth fly, particularly around downed logs, branches, roots and stumps that create protective recesses for fish. This is my main fly for extracting fish from such snaggy areas. To approach a snag from above, position yourself to allow a cast up-current from the target, feed line, and direct the rod tip to allow the Girdle Bug to drift into the snag as far as you judge possible; then twitch retrieve. The white legs are very visible, so it's easy to follow the position of your fly. Below a snag, cast to the eddies and slack water and twitch retrieve. This fly is fun to fish because it "moves" a lot of trout. The smaller size (14), like the Gray Leech (page 11), is good with light fly rods in small streams. The Girdle Bug is a good fly in spring, summer and fall when the fish are active.

Mayfly Nymphs

Olive Nymph ★

Hook: TMC® 3769—size 16, 18

Thread: Olive 8-0

Weight: Light

Tail: Wood duck flank fibers

Abdomen: Olive beaver

Rib: Fine copper wire

Wingcase: Olive goose biot

Thorax: Brown Australian opossum

Tying Notes: Weight the hook with a few turns of .010 at the thorax. The tail should be short, the abdomen thin and the thorax should be picked out and slightly bulging. The beaver, without guard hairs, allows very thin dubbing. A very durable fly. I carry dozens of these.

Fishing Notes:

This pattern was tied in response to the pumped stomach samplings of large numbers of trout, especially in the spring creeks where it is my most-used sub-surface pattern—fished with a fine tippet, usually 6X a bit of added weight and a small indicator. Over smooth water, I use moldable lead applied to the tippet about six inches above the fly. Taper the lead to a thin spindle—this will enter the water without the disturbance of lead shot. (Moldable lead has other advantages over shot: it doesn't slide down your tippet as easily; you can use the exact amount necessary; it doesn't snag as often; it comes off easily and is reusable. A disadvantage is that it needs to be checked periodically to make sure it's "well applied"—also, it's not the best in cold conditions.) The fluorescent red roll-on strike indicator is placed roughly an arm-span above the fly and should be just large enough to allow visibility. Roll-on indicators can easily be "downsized" by pinching off the excess. Sometimes, under demanding conditions, I'll use a small white indicator if I feel that the trout have become conditioned to the red.

The Olive Nymph is good in all kinds of water: riffles, runs, pools and man-made structures. It is at its best in the drop-offs and troughs of riffles for feeding fish. I've had some impressive hook-ups in this situation. The size 18 was responsible for 35 trout on Montana's Armstrong's Spring Creek one cloudy September day.

Another effective application of the Olive Nymph is as the trailing fly of a two-fly system—usually tied behind a scud or Dark-Ribbed Yellow Nymph. (See photo, page 20.)

Dark-Ribbed Yellow Nymph

Hook: TMC® 3761—size 14, 16

Thread: Yellow 6-0, 8-0

Weight: Light to medium

Tail: 3 or 4 pheasant tail fibers

Abdomen: Light yellow—I prefer Synthetic Living Fiber® (SLF) finesse

Rib: Thick black or brown floss

Wingcase: Dark turkey

Thorax: Light or natural Hare's Ear Plus®

Tying Notes: A straightforward, standard nymph tie. The weight is wrapped at the thorax, tail kept fairly short and the thorax is picked out. Randall Kaufmann's books, The Fly Tyer's Nymph Manual *and* Tying Nymphs, *are excellent references for nymph-tying instructions.*

Fishing Notes:

The Dark-Ribbed Yellow Nymph is another pattern designed from stomach pump contents and is especially useful in May and June, when trout are seeing sulphurs, yellow craneflies, and yellow stoneflies. It was responsible for a 50-trout day on Timber Coulee in southwest Wisconsin. It is fished in the standard nymph fashion, cast upstream and drifted into likely areas, usually with extra weight and an indicator. The Dark-Ribbed Yellow is an excellent upper fly of a two-fly system, combined with the Olive Nymph or small caddis/midge larva. The Dark-Ribbed Yellow has been in my armamentarium for about five years, and I find myself using it more and more throughout the season, especially on the spring creeks. On freestone streams, it is a good Little Yellow Stonefly imitation.

The author's son, Nathan, releasing a 22-inch rainbow trout on Wisconsin's Big Green River. The fish was feeding in a riffle and took a size 18 Olive Nymph trailing 10 inches behind a Dark-Ribbed Yellow.

Pheasant Tail Nymph

Hook: TMC® 3761—size 12 through 20

Thread: Brown 8-0, 6-0

Weight: Light to medium

Tail: Pheasant tail fibers

Abdomen: Pheasant tail fibers (forward extension of tail), wrapped around tying thread to reinforce

Rib: Fine or medium copper wire

Wingcase: Can use pheasant tail fibers, but I prefer rust goose biot on smaller sizes, narrow dark turkey on larger sizes

Thorax: Brown Australian opossum

Tying Notes: The "P.T." is universally known. Originally tied by Frank Sawyer, an English riverkeeper, using only copper wire and pheasant tail fibers, it now exists in a multitude of variations. Like the Olive Nymph, it is tied with weight at the thorax, a short tail and a picked-out thorax. I carry these by the dozen.

Pheasant Tail Soft-Hackle

Hook: Same as Pheasant Tail Nymph, favor size 16

Thread: Brown 6-0, 8-0

Weight: None

Abdomen and Rib: Same as nymph

Thorax: Gray muskrat with a bit of yellow SLF finesse

Hackle: Dun soft hackle

Tying Notes: The abdomen should be thin and the thorax just a slight bulge. Tie in a hen neck hackle by the tip, take 1 or 2 turns and tie off. (See Figure 4). Soft-hackle patterns are sparse ties.

Fishing Notes:

The Pheasant Tail Nymph is a classic general mayfly nymph, representative of a variety of species—Stenonema sp. in larger sizes, sulphurs and olives in mid and small sizes.

This pattern can be used in most sub-surface situations. I particularly like to use the P.T. Nymph when fishing man-made structures common on many midwestern streams. (See Figures 5, 6, 7 and photos, Colorplate 2.) Small trout are always "out and about" in the pools and slack water associated with structures, particularly in the tail end areas. The larger trout, unless they are actively feeding in the riffles above the structure, will often be lying beneath the undercut of the structure, especially near its head. Starting at the lower reaches of the structure, work your way gradually upstream, trying to present the fly so that it can be seen by trout tucked beneath the undercut. This usually means added weight and an indicator, casting your line so that it lands parallel and close to the bank over the structure. Often, there is a surface "foam line" visible in the current (see photo, Colorplate 2), which represents the main current flow. This foam line is the "conveyor belt" of floating and sub-surface insects and is where your indicator should be. With proper mending, you'll ensure a natural drift of your nymph along the currents that the sheltered trout are watching for food items. On smooth water surfaces, remember that the fly line will spook fish as it lands—cast gently and move upstream no more than one leader-length at a time. On choppy or discolored water, the fly line spooks fewer fish.

When larger trout decide to feed actively, they will often move upstream from the depths of the structures into the riffles. Here, they will lie just below the drop-off of the riffle or in deeper channels or troughs in the riffle. Sometimes these deeper channels are very subtle, but the trout will use them and you need to work these areas carefully with your fly. These deeper "slots" appear just a bit darker than the surrounding water. As with the Olive Nymph, I have taken many nice fish feeding upstream from their sheltering lies on P.T.s.

The Pheasant Tail Soft-Hackle is another effective imitator of a variety of insects—from caddis to sulphurs. The webby-hackle is the key to soft-hackle success, undulating to simulate a life-like appearance. It is best fished up and across with short to medium casts, allowing the fly to sink naturally without drag—simply lifting your rod tip as the fly drifts toward you is

---

Figure 4:

Soft-hackle feather

Soft-hackle feather ready for tie-in. It is tied in where the fibers have been spread, the tip trimmed and the butt grasped with the hackle pliers. Only 1 or 2 turns are needed.

the easiest way to take up drag-producing slack (Leisenring lift). Then, lower the rod tip and hold it stationary as the fly drifts downstream from your position. At the end of the drift, the fly will rise and the webby-hackles will close down over the body. The fly should rise in front of the suspected lie of the fish. Hopefully, the trout will think it is an ascending natural.

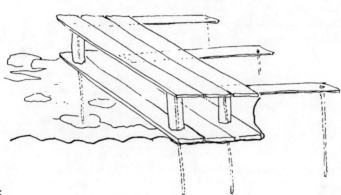

Figure 5:

Cross section of man-made "lunker" structure. These structures are designed to provide overhead bank cover for trout. Heavy machinery is used to install them—usually in series on the outside bend of the stream. They are held in place by reinforcing bars driven into the streambed and by large quarry rock placed on the top. Earth is then filled in over the rocks and the area is seeded. In a matter of months, the streambank returns to a natural appearance. Trout quickly take up residence beneath the overhead cover.

Figure 6:

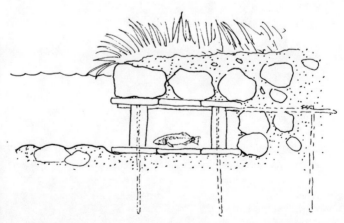

Cross section of man-made structure in place. The depth is generally thigh to waist level, but it can be deeper. Getting your sub-surface imitations down to trout eye level is important. They will flash out from beneath the structure to take food items. If they are on the lookout for surface food, they will position themselves so that they can see insects drifting just off the grassy overhangs. Cast your dry patterns close to the bank.

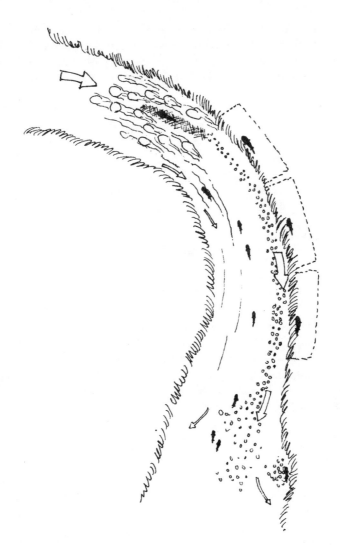

Figure 7:

Top view of three structures (dotted lines) in series on the outer curve of stream. Note foam line (small circles). Heavy current=wide arrows; quieter current=narrow arrows; deep slot=crosshatched area in riffle above structure. Inner curve is shallow; outer curve in area of structures has good depth. The largest trout often take cover under the uppermost structure and will feed in the deep slot in the riffle—look for it. Feeding activity is important along the inside border of the foam line where there is a seam of faster/slower current. Smaller trout are more likely in the tail area. In later summer when the grass is high, large trout may move to inside of curve and watch for terrestrials. Also, look for fish beneath collections of foam. The grass along the structures is an important dry fly drift area.

COLORPLATE 1

Gray Leech
p. 11

Wooly Bugger
p. 12

Clouser Deep Minnow
p. 13

Black Ghost
p. 15

Girdle Bug
p. 18

Muddler Minnow
p. 14

San Juan Worm
p. 17

Foreground: A completed structure ready for placement.
Background: Lumber and quarry rock, the raw materials of structures.
This stream improvement project involved Rullands Coulee, a tributary of
Timber Coulee.

A newly installed "structure" on Timber Coulee. The man-made structures
lie beneath the heavy rock. Note the small riffle upstream and the foam line.

MAYFLY NYMPHS

Olive Nymph
p. 19

Dark-Ribbed
Yellow Nymph
p. 20

Pheasant Tail
Nymph
p. 21

Pheasant Tail
Soft-Hackle
p. 21

Gold-Ribbed
Hare's-Ear
p. 25

(black)

(olive)

Small Black, Olive Nymph
p. 26

Hexagenia Nymph
p. 27

Black Stonefly
Nymph
p. 28

Dragonfly Nymph
p. 29

Prince Nymph
p. 31

Tan p. 32

Olive p. 32

Peeking p. 32

Olive Lace p. 33

Chartreuse p. 32

Metallic Green p. 34

CADDIS LARVAE

nge Scud
p. 35

Olive-Gray Scud p. 36

Cress Bug
p. 37

Soft-Hackle
Sow Bug
p. 38

Pass Lake Wet
p. 39

COLORPLATE 4

Photo—Herb Weigl

This 27-inch wild brown trout took a size 12 Black Ghost on Pennsylvania's Le Tort.

Photo—John Shillinglaw

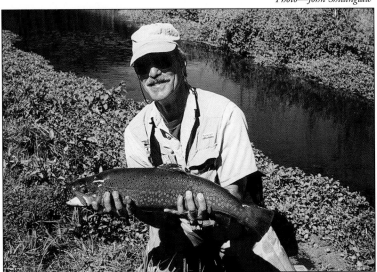

A 27-inch brown trout from a southwestern Wisconsin spring creek. The fish took a size 14 Pass Lake Wet Fly fished as shown in Figure 3. This was a brood-stock fish from a catch and release stream. Note the heron "peck mark" on the head.

Gold-Ribbed Hare's Ear

Hook: TMC® 3761—size 10, 12, 14

Thread: Brown 6-0

Weight: Medium at thorax

Tail: Hare's mask fibers with underfur removed or pheasant tail fibers, tan marabou in size 10

Abdomen: Fine hare's ear

Rib: Gold tinsel

Wingcase: Dark turkey; can use strip of Mylar®, or Lure-Flash® Translucent

Thorax: Coarse hare's ear, picked out

Tying Notes: This is another straightforward nymph tie; again, see Kaufmann's The Fly Tyer's Nymph Manual. This tie is virtually identical to Kaufmann's tie. The Mylar strip or lure-flash wingcase creates a "flash back" that is occasionally useful. I favor a "spiky" look created by picking out the hare's ear fibers of the abdomen and thorax.

Fishing Notes:

This is another classic, versatile nymph pattern useful as a general imitator of larger mayflies. The size 10 fly represents brown drakes. The undulating marabou simulates the movement of the ascending nymph. The size 12 and 14 represent the Stenonemas. Size 14 in darker shades imitate Hendricksons and in grayer shades represent the gray drake. The Gold-Ribbed Hare's Ear is a good choice as a "searching" nymph on streams where these larger mayflies are found, especially during the various emergence periods.

Small Black Nymph

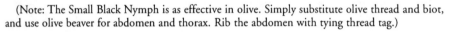

Hook: TMC® 3761—size 18, 20; TMC 2487—size 20, 22

Thread: Black 8-0

Weight: None, or few turns of .010 at thorax

Tail: Black goose biot tip

Abdomen: Black Krystal Flash®

Thorax: Black mole or black ostrich herl

Wingcase: Goose biot; same as tail

(Note: The Small Black Nymph is as effective in olive. Simply substitute olive thread and biot, and use olive beaver for abdomen and thorax. Rib the abdomen with tying thread tag.)

Tying Notes: I usually use just enough weight to break surface tension. Tie in goose biot tail; just a very short length of tip is needed. Tie in black Krystal Flash, wind tying thread up to thorax area over remaining biot, wind Krystal Flash abdomen and tie off. Trim the Krystal Flash and bend the remaining biot back, out of the way to allow for dubbing a "dot" of mole at thorax. Pull remaining biot over thorax, snip, and whip finish.

Fishing Notes:

This is a good fly for difficult spring creek fish, like those of Black Earth Creek near Madison, Wisconsin, especially during Trico or Pseudocloeon time. If it appears that the fish are surface feeding yet a dry pattern is ineffective, strongly consider the Small Black or Olive Nymph, either trailing about 18 inches behind a small Parachute Adams (page 90) or with a small indicator a few feet above the fly. A 7X tippet is called for in this situation; the nymph is cast as delicately as a dry fly. A lightweight, progressive taper, two or three-weight rod is an excellent choice for this kind of fishing. See the chapter "Nymphing the Film" in Gary Borger's book *Nymphing*.

I can't tell you how many times I've pumped trout and found large numbers of tiny dark "nymphs." The Small Black and Olive Nymphs are the ones to use in this situation. To fish the smaller nymphs deeply, tie them about 10 inches behind a larger scud or nymph pattern. Use a 6X or 7X tippet tied to the hook bend of the larger fly. Extra weight is usually necessary and an indicator is used. You'll be amazed how often good-sized fish take the smaller fly.

Carry dozens of these—they don't take up much space.

Hexagenia Nymph

Hook: Mustad® 9672—size 6, 8

Thread: Yellow 6-0

Weight: Medium

Tail: Gray-yellow or tan marabou

Abdomen: Pale yellow Synthetic Living Fiber® (SLF) mixed
   50-50 with red fox underfur

Rib: Yellow tying thread

Wingcase: Dark turkey

Thorax: Same as abdomen, picked out

Hackle Legs: Gray partridge soft hackle or amber wood duck flank fibers

Tying Notes: This is an easier tie than the "wiggle nymph" and has better hooking properties. The marabou tail should be long enough to undulate when fished. A dubbing loop makes tying the abdomen easier. To imitate the legs, after dubbing thorax, tie in gray partridge or wood duck fiber tips forward over the hook eye; then take half the fibers and fold back to the far side of the shank and secure with thread. Repeat with the remaining fibers to the near side of the shaft; add a bit of dubbing if needed, then pull over wingcase and whip finish. Brush the body with Velcro®.

Fishing Notes:

   The famous adult form of this mayfly will be discussed later (page 62). The nymph has a period of usefulness that includes a portion of the season much longer than the adult. The Hex nymphs can be fished in early evening, before the adults appear during the emergence periods in June (southern and central Midwest) and late June to early July (northern areas). They are a favored food item of trout living in streams with populations of Hexagenia limbata. I've seen trout absolutely stuffed with these nymphs, stomachs bulging and nymphs coming out of their mouths on the Willow River of central Wisconsin. The insects favor streams with silty areas; such streams usually have less gradient and slower current and tend to meander. On the outside corner of the meanders, an undercut develops, providing good trout holding water.

   To fish the nymph, position yourself on the inside corner of a meander, cast up and across to the opposite bank and let the fly drift through the undercut area, giving an occasional twitch. Strip-retrieve at the end of the drift. If overhanging brush covers the holding water, position yourself upstream and on the same side of the undercut and cast the nymph as already described for the Black Ghost (Figure 3). These simple techniques have become a stand-by for me during early May on the sand country streams of central Wisconsin—the Willow, White, Pine and Mecan rivers.

Stonefly Nymphs

Little Yellow Stonefly

See Dark-Ribbed Yellow Nymph (page 20).

Black Stonefly

Hook: Mustad® 9672—size 6, 8, 10; TMC® 3761—size 16, 18

Thread: Black 6-0

Weight: Medium to heavy, flattened

Tail: 2 black goose biots, splayed horizontally on size 6, 8, 10; moose hair on size 16, 18

Abdomen: Black Hare's Ear Plus®, trimmed

Rib: Larva Lace® nymph rib, black on large sizes; black floss on smaller sizes

Wingcase: Dark turkey; coated with head cement

Thorax and legs: Black calf tail in dubbing loop for size 6, 8, 10; Hare's Ear Plus for size 16, 18

Tying Notes: This is another straightforward nymph tie. Because the Black Stonefly is fished deeply and prone to loss, I am not overly concerned with details such as a double or triple wingcase when tying them. Tie a few unweighted imitations for use when the nymphs migrate toward shore to emerge.

Fishing Notes:

The fly fisher will find that trout feeding on large dark stonefly nymphs is a much more common experience than trout feeding on the adults.

The larger Black Stonefly Nymph is a good year-round pattern in large, rocky streams such as Wisconsin's Wolf River, portions of Minnesota's Root River, and many Upper Peninsula streams. For these situations, I like to use a 9-foot, 6-weight, stiff rod with a hefty tippet and added weight. Work upstream, casting slightly across current and up just enough to let the fly sink to the bottom near likely holding areas, mending as necessary to control drag. Let the fly complete the drift by swinging below you. Let it trail in the water; then directly flip it upstream again (tension cast). Try to avoid a lot of casting action with heavy flies and keep your loops open. As with most nymph fishing, if you're not bumping bottom occasionally, add weight. This is also a good steelhead pattern on Great Lakes tributary streams.

The smaller sizes of the Black Stonefly are good choices for winter nymphing on streams with cobble and gravel bottoms.

Dragonfly Nymph

Hook: Mustad® 9672—size 6

Thread: Olive 6-0

Weight: Medium, at rear of hook

Eyes: 2 small black glass beads (size 11/0) threaded on monofilament (10- or 12-pound test) and tied to hook

Body: Dark olive sculpin wool and dark olive SLF

Hackle: Olive-dyed grizzly marabou, trimmed on top; head cement applied in area of wingcase

Tying Notes: Weight is applied to rear half of the shank. The two glass beads are threaded onto monofilament. The monofilament is bent with the "tag ends" running back along the shank and the beads in "eye position" near the hook eye. Tie monofilament to shank and criss-cross the thread between the eyes to secure them. (See Figure 8.) Run the thread to the rear of the hook and form a dubbing loop. For the body dubbing, cut a three-quarters-inch section from a rope of sculpin wool and tease the fibers apart gently without disturbing their parallel alignment. When you have enough fibers teased from the rope section, lay SLF fibers on the wool (see Figure 9), apply the dubbing material to the loop, spin and dub the body.

Brush the body fibers out to each side; then trim to the "flattened" Dragonfly Nymph shape: wide in middle and tapering toward the hook bend. Trim top and bottom, leaving a wide hook gap on bottom. Take one turn of grizzly-dyed marabou for hackle, just behind eye, tie off marabou, trim on top and apply head cement over the trimmed marabou to simulate a wing-case. Whip finish in front of eye. Dorsal segmentation can be suggested with black felt tip pen. Jewelry spacers, small dumbbell-shaped springs available in craft stores, may also be used to represent eyes on the Dragonfly Nymph and other patterns such as Wooly Buggers (page 12).

Fishing Notes:

Looking back over old fishing notes is fun, especially in mid-winter. My notes from May 4, 1975 state, "We found lots of brown-black stoneflies and olive-black dragonfly nymphs in the trouts' bellies." These notes were made on the Wolf River. Larger rivers in the northern areas of the upper Midwest—the Namekagon, Brule, White, Ontonagon and Escanaba—have good Dragonfly Nymph populations and as noted, a lot of them end up in "trouts' bellies." Fish them deep, like the Stonefly Nymph, with added weight.

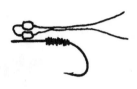

Figure 8:

Two black beads are threaded onto monofilament. The beads are placed in the "eye position" and monofilament "tag ends" tied to shank. The thread is then criss-crossed between the beads.

Figure 9:

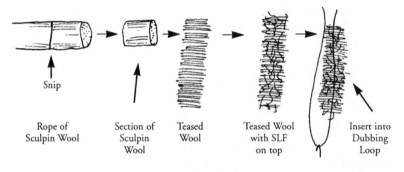

| Rope of Sculpin Wool | Section of Sculpin Wool | Teased Wool | Teased Wool with SLF on top | Insert into Dubbing Loop |

Snip

Camping on the Little Wolf River, Wisconsin.

Peacock Nymphs

Prince Nymph

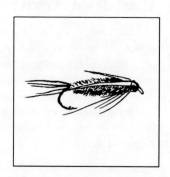

Hook: TMC® 3761—size 10, 14; TMC 5263—size 10

Thread: Black 6-0

Weight: Medium to heavy

Tail: 2 brown goose biots or pheasant tail fibers

Body: Peacock

Wing: White goose biots in "V" flat over back

Hackle: Soft brown hackle

Tying Notes: The two tail biots are splayed horizontally. The peacock herl is reinforced by winding it around the tying thread and then winding it forward. The hackle is applied and the wing biots are tied in a "V" over the hackle and body.

I will often omit the tail on the Prince because a similar nymph, the Brown-Hackle Peacock (BHP), favored by Dennis Graupe of Spring Creek Anglers in Coon Valley, Wisconsin, has no tail and is excellently effective.

An optional brass bead at the head adds weight and "flash" and is sometimes preferred by deep-lying trout.

Fishing Notes:

There is great value in fishing peacock-bodied nymphs—they are good fish catchers. The Zug Bug and Brown-Hackle Peacock (BHP) are essentially equivalent to the Prince Nymph. I favor the white biot wings—if you feel they are too much dressing for the situation, they may be trimmed while you are on-stream.

I view the Prince Nymph as an attractor nymph and fish it when I want to fish deep but am uncertain what the trout are feeding on. The Prince is useful on all types of water.

The size 10 pattern is useful, fished with action, during periods of Isonychia activity.

Larvae

Caddis Larvae

Caddis larvae are found year-round in our streams and are discussed in this section. The pupae, emergers and adults are discussed in the SEASONAL caddis section.

If you examine a rock removed from the stream bed, you'll probably find both cased and uncased caddis larvae. The uncased crawling larvae will be of varying colors: from cream, to olive, to bright green. The cased larvae are enveloped in cases of vegetable material or pebbles attached to the substrate. Both kinds of caddis larvae are very important food items for trout. The larvae will either be taken as they drift or actively "rooted" from underwater twigs and stones.

Caddis Larva, Olive (Tan, Chartreuse)

Hook: TMC® 2457—size 14, 16

Thread: Olive 6-0

Weight: Medium

Body: Olive Antron®, or SLF finesse approximating BCS 30; also use tan dubbing to approximate BCS 55 and chartreuse

Rib: Pearlescent Krystal Flash® or fine copper wire

Head: Dark brown Australian opossum or black Hare's Ear Plus®, picked out

Tying Notes: Caddis larvae are extremely easy to tie. Simply dub and rib the body, then add a small dubbed head. As an option, a black glass bead or brass bead may be added to the olive and tan larvae. The Chartreuse Caddis Larva is tied down to size 20 on a TMC 2487 hook.

*To tie the common cased larva (**Peeking Caddis**), use brown SLF dubbing on the rear two-thirds of the shank and trim the fibers fairly short. Then add a short bit of creamy tan or light green dubbing in front of the SLF to represent the encased larva. Use brown Australian opossum for head and pick out fibers to represent legs.*

Fishing Notes:

Most midwestern streams support good populations of Caddis Larvae. Be sure to look for them and tie suitable imitations if the patterns given here are not a good match. Judging from stomach pump samples, the larval imitations are useful year-round. Olive larvae predominate in stomach samplings.

Fish the Olive, Tan and Peeking Caddis deeply with added weight and an indicator. These larval imitations are some of my most-used sub-surface patterns, particularly in April and May. The Tan Caddis Larva may also be used to represent a Cranefly Larva (page 70).

I'm not certain what the Chartreuse Larva represents, but the trout seem to know. It seems most effective on streams in the Coulee country of Iowa, Minnesota and Wisconsin. It is fished in the same manner as the Olive Larva.

Olive Lace Larva (Trout candy)

Hook: TMC® 2487—size 16

Thread: Olive 6-0

Weight: None

Body: Olive Larva Lace®, hollow

Rib: Tying thread

Head: Small dubbed "dot" of dark brown Australian opossum

Tying Notes: Start the thread at hook bend, wrapping it firmly. Then "feed" a short length of hollow Larva Lace over the hook eye, down the shaft, leaving a short length of shaft bare near the eye for the head. Rib the Larva Lace with tying thread. This creates an effective segmented result and represents both caddis and midge larvae. An alternative tying method involves simply winding the shank with thread the intended color of the body; then over-winding the thread with clear midge lace.

Fishing Notes:

The Olive Lace Larva is an excellent choice as the trailing fly of a two-fly system. (See Figure 10.) Using a 6X tippet, tie it about 10 inches behind a larger nymph or scud pattern and fish it in the deeper runs and drop-offs of riffles. This technique recently produced a rainbow of over 23 inches in southwest Wisconsin.

Fished alone, the Olive Lace Larva is good in shallow riffles and smaller streams. It enters the water without much disturbance, sinks fairly well without added weight and has a realistic appearance.

Metallic Green Caddis Larva

Hook: TMC® 2487—size 16, 18, 20

Thread: Black 8-0

Weight: None

Body: Green Krystal Flash® or metallic green thread, Sulky® brand

Hackle: Starling

Head: Black mole

Tying Notes: This is another easy fly to tie. Simply wind the abdomen with a few strands of Krystal Flash or Sulky thread, add one or two turns of starling neck hackle, swept back and dub the head.

Fishing Notes:

The Metallic Green Caddis Larva is used during the Black Caddis emergence period (see Hatch Chart, page 94), when there are no adults on the water. This fly is a Bighorn River transplant that is most often used trailing behind a Soft-Hackle Sow Bug (page 38), with extra weight and an indicator. The Metallic Green (or the chartreuse) patterns are good options to try if the Olive Caddis Larva is not particularly effective.

Midge Larvae

Midge larvae may be fished either in the film or more deeply. They are discussed in the midge section of Surface and Film Flies (page 40).

Figure 10:

Two-Fly System

Scuds and Cress Bugs

Scuds and cress bugs are vegetation-loving crustaceans found in limestone spring creeks of high water quality. Scuds (freshwater shrimp) exist in a variety of colors, and individuals change color after molting. Cress bugs are gray with a black line across their "backbone." Both scuds and cress bugs have a dorsal chitinous "shell" and are segmented. Scuds are flattened vertically, cress bugs horizontally. No matter how they are flattened or what color they are, trout love them and will rummage around in the cress and "weed" seeking them out. Trout are so fond of them that they will eat the imitation, even in streams where the naturals don't exist (probably mistaking it for an egg or part of a crayfish). I always carry a good supply of imitations, a couple of which are transplants from the Bighorn River—the Bighorn Scud and the Soft-Hackle Sow Bug.

Orange (Bighorn) Scud ★

Hook: TMC® 2457 or Dai-Riki® 135—size 10, 12, 14

Thread: Orange 6-0

Weight: Heavy

Tail: Few strands of orange Krystal Flash® or orange dyed pheasant tail

Body: Orange SLF® mixed with orange dyed rabbit, 50-50 mix

Over Body: Thin strip from freezer bag or thin strip of clear stretch elastic (from fabric store)

Rib: Red copper wire

Tying and Fishing Notes: See Olive-Gray Scud, page 36.

Olive-Gray Scud

Hook: TMC® 2457—size 12, 14, 16

Thread: Olive or gray 6-0

Weight: Heavy

Tail: Pearlescent Krystal Flash® or gray goose

Body: SLF®, olive and gray mixed; can add chopped Zelon® and/or snowshoe hare's foot fibers; color range from BCS 31 to BCS 104

Overbody: Stretch elastic, clear

Rib: Copper wire

Tying Notes: Get organized to tie a dozen flies: mix the dubbing, cut the elastic strips and ribbing wire and weight a dozen hooks. Then take four to five strands of Krystal Flash and tie in tail down low on the hook bend, trim tail and set aside remaining Krystal Flash to be used on the next fly. Tie in ribbing wire and elastic strip; then form a dubbing loop, insert dubbing and twist loop. A rotary vise is very handy for advancing the dubbing loop forward. Leave a little space behind hook eye and tie off the loop. Bring the elastic strip over the back and tie down. Then advance the ribbing (rotary vise is excellent here, also) to give a distinct segmented look and tie off. Pick out the dubbing on the underside of the fly, trying to conceal the point and barb with picked-out fibers. Brush back the picked out dubbing with Velcro® and you're done.

Fishing Notes:

Freshwater shrimp exhibit wide color variation—the orange and olive-gray are my favored colors for the imitations—pink and tan are also good. As has previously been mentioned, scuds apply to all streams at all times.

On an April trip to Minnesota, fly-fishing DNR personnel at the Lanesboro headquarters recommended two patterns: "Baetis nymphs and Orange Scuds." The Orange Scuds worked beautifully on the south fork of the Root River.

A particularly good situation to use a scud is in deep pools of heavily fished streams. Cast to the head of the pool and let the fly sink to the eye level of the trout lying on the bottom—scuds get deep in a hurry, but take your time and let the fish "recover from the cast"—then slowly strip in line and wiggle the rod tip.

Scuds are also good choices for the "deep dapping" technique over man-made structures or deep undercuts. They are not particularly good over glassy, smooth water surfaces because they land with too much of a "plop" and frighten fish. In this situation try to cast to the riffled water upcurrent from the quiet water and allow the scud to drift into the target water, or cast directly into the smooth water, let the fly settle, and wait for the fish to recover as previously mentioned. On rare occasion, the "plop" of a scud over smooth water will trigger a response from large feeding fish. I've experienced this response with a sighted 22-inch brown trout that refused careful dry fly presentations but turned and instantly took a scud which plopped one foot behind it.

Cress Bug

Hook: TMC® 3769—size 14, 16

Thread: Gray

Weight: Light, flattened

Body: Gray Antron® to approximate BCS 104, add a touch of Pearlescent Spectrablend®

Overbody: Thin strip cut from freezer bag or Mylar®

Dorsal Stripe: 1 strand of black Krystal Flash® pulled over overbody

Ribbing: Fine copper

Tying Notes: An important element of this imitation is the horizontal flattening, accomplished by picking out the dubbing on the sides only, trimming any protruding dubbing on the bottom and crimping with a small flat-nose pliers.

Fishing Notes:

Cress bugs are favored food items of trout in streams of high water quality such as the Little Green in southwest Wisconsin. Although good throughout all seasons, cress bugs are a good choice during the summer fished through channels in the "weed" (see photo, Colorplate 14) when surface activity is lacking. Examine a sample of "cress" or "weed" from the stream you are fishing. If cress bugs are present, you can be sure the trout will be feeding on them.

Soft-Hackle Sow Bug

Hook: TMC® 3769—size 14, 16

Thread: Gray 6-0

Weight: None

Body: Haretron® cinnamon caddis dubbing

Rib: Tying thread tag

Hackle: Soft gray hen hackle or partridge

Head: Several turns of red tying thread, cemented for a glossy finish

Tying Notes: The Soft-Hackle Sow Bug is easy to tie. See Kaufmann's The Fly Tyer's Nymph Manual for detailed instructions on hackling. The red head seems to be an important attracting feature. The soft hackles should be tied trailing back around the body. (See Figure 4.)

Fishing Notes:

This is another Bighorn River transplant that is most often used as the upper, attracting fly of a two-fly system, with the trailing fly being either a caddis larva, pupa or a midge pattern. The Sow Bug does its job getting the trout to "take a look," then take the lower fly.

Soft-hackled flies, of course, are effective on their own, mimicking emergers or drowned adults of a variety of insects. There are hundreds of soft-hackled patterns—the Soft-Hackle Sow Bug and Pheasant Tail Soft-Hackle (page 21)—are two of my favorites.

This fly and similar flies, such as the Blue-Winged Olive Wet-Dry (page 48) and the Partridge and Yellow Soft-Hackle (page 70) may be fished upstream, like a dry fly, to "bulging" trout. They also may be fished downstream like a wet fly or beneath the surface utilizing the Leisenring lift.

Ron Manz, of Wisconsin Rapids, Wisconsin, is a lifelong fly fisher of great experience and skill. One of his all-time favorite flies is a pattern called the **March Brown Soft-Hackle**. Ron uses a TMC 200R hook, size 14 and light orange tying thread. The body is a mix of hare's ear and squirrel dubbed with a loop and ribbed with copper. The soft hackle is two turns of brown partridge. Ron notes that the pattern is effective on most streams, fished down and across with "mini" twitches.

Wet Flies

Pass Lake Wet Fly ★

Hook: TMC® 3761—size 14, 16

Thread: Black 6-0, 8-0

Weight: Light

Tail: Mallard flank or golden pheasant crest

Body: Fine black chenille or peacock herl

Hackle: Soft brown hackle

Wing: White calf tail or calf body hair

Tying Notes: The Pass Lake Wet Fly is a straightforward pattern to tie. The hackle is tied in as the Soft-Hackle Sow Bug; then the calf hair is tied in last—over the hackle, angling back over the body.

Fishing Notes:

The original Pass Lake is a Wisconsin fly, designed by a Clintonville minister in 1938 and popularized by his son-in-law, Earl Paape. Earl notes that the fly was originally tied, unweighted with mallard flank, black chenille, brown hackle and white calf tail in front of hackle. This was fished as a "damp" fly, with the chenille soaking up water and pulling it under a bit. Earl has tied and fished many variations of the fly but still favors the original dressing except for the wing, which he placed behind the hackle. My preference is to tie two separate versions: a wet fly, usually weighted, using peacock herl and pheasant crest, and a dry pattern, presented later (page 91).

The Pass Lake Wet has not been dislodged from my fly box for over 30 years. It is most often fished in the wet fly style—cast across and down (like a small Black Ghost, page 15), slowly swinging in the current and twitch retrieving. The pattern is especially good for probing the upper end of man-made structures. Stand upstream and drift the fly (extra weight is often needed) into the water at the head of the structure. Let it hang in the current, twitching up a bit, and let it fall back down-current again, keeping it in the water a long time as you slowly proceed downstream. The white wing allows good visibility so that you can keep track of the fly's position. The Pass Lake is very good in the brush, using short, accurate casts into openings, directing the fly around snags with your rod tip. It is made to order for streams like Michigan's Pigeon River.

This fly is fun to fish and its popularity is well-deserved.

Surface and Film Flies

Midges

At last we're getting into a year-round fly with a surface pattern—the midge. Being able to fish "small" is of critical importance on many of our midwestern streams— particularly in heavily fished areas. Many trout learn they are often safer choosing small food items, different from lures, spinners, night crawlers and size 14 elk hair caddis. The midge patterns presented here are simple and represent a very workable collection of larvae through adults. Though small, they are easily tied and you can carry a lot of them—they don't take up much space. My 2 1/2 x 3 1/2-inch swing leaf fly box holds most of the midge patterns, plus Tricos and Pseudocloeon.

Please refer to Midge Larvae Chart (small caddis larva, blackfly larvae, and tiny mayfly nymphs will be represented by this assortment as well).

MIDGE LARVAE CHART

HOOK	SIZE	BODY	HEAD	NOTES
DAIICHI 1140	18, 20, 22	Black Krystal Flash® Green Krystal Flash® Yellow beaver	Black mole Black mole Black mole	Tie yellow in size 22 only
TMC 101	22	Olive biot	Olive beaver	
TMC 2487	16, 18	Fine copper wire including red and green	Black mole or Hare's Ear Plus	"Brassies"
TMC 200R	20	Tan Antron® BCS55 with fine gold rib	Tan tying thread	
TMC 2487	16	Red Hollow Larva Lace®	Black tying thread	Same as olive lace larva (Trout candy)

Tying Notes: The midge larvae are quick and easy to tie—no weight—no tails. The fur heads are just "dots." Keep the fur and Antron bodies thin and tight. For Krystal Flash bodies, use one or two strands for small sizes, three or four strands for larger sizes. Use 8-0 thread except on the Red Larva Lace (trout candy) imitation on which Red 6-0 is used to secure the lace.

Fishing Notes:

If you know the stream you're fishing has a good midge population (stomach pump sampling or clouds of midges over the water), you need to consider fishing them, particularly if your fishing with larger mayfly or caddisfly imitations has been slow.

In the morning, with no fish bulging or rising, use a midge larva imitation tied on a 6X or 7X tippet behind a larger weighted nymph with an indicator, fished in, and just below the riffles. I usually start with the green or black Krystal Flash version.

continued on page 41

COLORPLATE 5
——— MIDGE PATTERNS ———

Black

Yellow

Red Lace

Dark p. 41

Green

Olive

Olive

Gray Pullover
p. 42

Tan

"Brassies"

MIDGE LARVAE See chart, p. 40   MIDGE PUPAE

Dark
p. 44

Medium
p. 44

Light
p. 44

Horizontal
p. 42

Vertical
p. 43

Dark
p. 41

MIDGE ADULTS

MIDGE EMERGERS

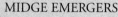

Griffith's Gnat
Variation
p. 45

Griffith's Gnat
Variation
p. 45

Fore and Aft Midge
p. 46

——— BLUE-WINGED OLIVE PATTERNS ———

Floating Nymph
p. 47

Wet-Dry
p. 48

No-Hackle Emerger
p. 49

Parachute
p. 50

Parachute
p. 50

Quill-Winged Olive
p. 52

COLORPLATE 6

A TRIO OF STREAMS

The "holy water" on Michigan's Au Sable.

Southwestern Wisconsin's Spring Coulee, a "neighbor" of Timber Coulee.

Central Wisconsin's Tomorrow River in mid-August during the Ephoron leukon hatch period. (See text, page 67).

COLORPLATE 7

—— MAYFLIES ——

Hendrickson Parachute
p. 54

Red Quill
p. 54

Hendrickson
Duck-Shoulder Dun
p. 55

Sulplhur Sparkle Dun
(tied by George Close)
p. 56

Sulplhur CDC Parachute
p. 57

Adams Hair-Wing
(tied by the late Ed Haaga)
p. 58

Close Carpet Fly
(tied by George Close)
p. 59

Gray Drake Parachute
p. 60

Light Cahill Parachute
p. 61

COLORPLATE 8

WINTER

A plump 10-incher demonstrates that trout feed well during the winter.

The Doc Smith branch of the Castle Rock in southwestern Wisconsin, a catch and release stream that holds large brown trout.

The Tan Antron imitation is very useful, fished alone, for fish feeding near the surface with no apparent insect activity. Fished without weight and with a micro-indicator, this fly has produced some excellent fishing. One morning in mid-March on Iowa's Spring Branch, it was the only fly the trout were eating, producing a dozen good-sized holdovers above the hatchery. I was using my short two-weight rod and 7X tippet, gently casting the larva like a dry fly.

The small "brassies" are my choice in deeper runs with a fair amount of current or in deep drop-offs below riffles. Cast them up into the shallow water, and let them tumble down the face of the drop-off, adding weight as necessary.

The larger black Krystal Flash/mole pattern may be used as a black fly larva in northern areas.

The tiny yellow and olive patterns were tied in response to pump samples from surface feeding spring creek trout. These imitations are fished like the Tan Antron Larva.

Dark Midge Pupa

Hook: Daiichi® 1140—size 20

Thread: Black 8-0

Abdomen: Black Krystal Flash®

Thorax: Gray beaver

Wingcase: White Antron® yarn fibers

Tying Notes: The Midge Pupa is essentially the same as the Larva (page 40), with the addition of the Antron, which is pulled over the thorax like a wingcase. After tying the wingcase down, whip finish; then snip the residual Antron so that it extends slightly in front of the hook eye.

To tie a DARK MIDGE EMERGER, simply add a tail of a few gray marabou fibers or a tuft of muskrat, length equal to abdomen.

Fishing Notes:

See Vertical Midge Emerger, page 43.

Gray Pullover

Hook: TMC® 101—size 22, 24

Thread: Black 8-0

Body: Gray muskrat or gray goose quill fiber

Overbody: Twinkle organza fibers

Tying Notes: This represents a pupa and is a straightforward tie. The organza is tied down at the hook bend, the body is completed and the organza is pulled over the entire body, wingcase style.

Fishing Notes:

See Vertical Midge Emerger, page 43.

Horizontal Midge Emerger

Hook: TMC® 101—size 24, 26

Thread: Black 8-0

Tail: Tuft of dark muskrat or marabou

Abdomen: Tying thread

Thorax: Gray muskrat

Hackle: Grizzly

Tying Notes: This is a pattern of Roger Hill of Colorado Springs, Colorado, designed for the South Platte. Roger describes the fly as a "size 26 Wooly Bugger." The thorax is just a slight bulge and the hackle is wound over the thorax only.

Vertical Midge Emerger

Hook: TMC® 101—size 22

Thread: Black 8-0

Body: Gray beaver

Rib: Pearlescent Krystal Flash®

Wing: White Antron® yarn

Hackle: Grizzly

Tying Notes: Tie in Antron yarn fibers, just behind the hook eye, extending straight forward. Trim the fibers extending to the rear. Dub a fine body and rib with Krystal Flash. Tie in small grizzly hackle and wind over the area of the wing butt; then wind tying thread at the hook eye so that it elevates the wing to about a 45-degree angle. Trim "wing" to proper length, slightly long.

Fishing Notes:

When treated with floatant, the wing of the Vertical Midge Emerger is very visible. I use this fly as an indicator in "touchy" situations, tying one of the pupae on 7X as a trailing fly.

I usually fish the Dark Pupa, Dark Emerger, and Gray Pullover singly to visibly feeding fish at the tails of riffles, casting from the side and slightly below the feeders. The tiny larval patterns are well worth a try in this situation also.

These patterns are often necessary on the "flats"—stretches of deep, quiet water where trout are often seen feeding leisurely, with dimpling rises, to "invisible" insects. There is so much that can go wrong trying to catch these fish—one mistake and they settle to the bottom and stop feeding. An even more frustrating scenario is when the trout are aware of your presence yet continue rising to everything but your fly. This is a signal that something needs to be changed—your fly, tippet or your approach—or maybe all three! Sometimes, just getting into casting position is a major task. If you're wading, don't "push" waves over the trout. Don't show the fish anything except the tippet and the fly—no rod or line flash and no line spray (tippets preferably are a bit sub-surface and crinkle-free). I prefer a visible pattern, such as a Midge Adult if possible, but usually a film pattern (Midge Pupa or Emerger) is needed. If you can't see the fly, watch floating sections of the leader next to the tippet. If the current is "non-existent," just let the pattern sit. Become part of the environment. If you see a trout inspect and refuse your fly, change flies and, if possible, go smaller. If the trout takes your fly—be extra happy!

Midge Adults

Dark Midge Adult

Hook: TMC® 101—size 20, 22, 24, 26

Thread: Black 8-0

Body: Black beaver or mole, thin

Hackle: Few turns of high quality black hackle

Medium Midge Adult

Hook: TMC® 101—size 20, 22, 24, 26

Thread: Gray 8-0

Body: Gray beaver, thin

Hackle: Grizzly

Light Midge Adult ★

Hook: TMC® 101—size 20, 22, 24, 26

Thread: Cream 8-0

Body: Light yellow beaver

Hackle: Cream

Tying Notes: These can be tied with a few strands of Lureflash® translucent lying over the body to represent a wing (I prefer wingless). I used to tie these with a tail (they are better tailless). For some reason, the simplest fly seems to be the best. These are easy to tie; simply dub a body and take a couple turns of hackle. The hackle fibers can be trimmed on the bottom as needed. I guarantee you'll need them—from the first "fishable" days of January through the year.

Fishing Notes:

The adult patterns are very useful, especially over quieter water. Visibility is quite good. One of my all-time favorite trout took a Light Midge Adult. The fish was sipping something small beneath overhanging box elder branches in a difficult casting situation on the west fork of the Kickapoo, in southwestern Wisconsin. I thought the fish was eating small beetles, but I wanted to use a more visible fly. I tied on a 7X tippet and drew it through my thumb and forefinger moistened with contact lens cleaner, then drew it through once more, fingers coated with "mud" to put the tippet sub-surface. The Light Midge was then tied on, being careful when tightening the knot not to cause any kinks. Next, a few practice casts in a safe area below the fish, then a few steps upstream and a good cast into the only opening in the overlying branches—a 1-foot drift—a rise, and I tightened. The fish ran upstream, and I moved up in front of the branches so that it couldn't get back to its secure area. The fish was landed and turned out to be an 18-inch brown trout. The stomach pump revealed it had been eating midges.

Griffith's Gnat (variation) ★

Hook: TMC® 100—size 16, 18; TMC 101—size 20, 22
Thread: Black 8-0
Body: Tying thread—add a touch of superglue; then wrap hackle
Hackle: Grizzly, high-quality, palmered full length

Griffith's Gnat (variation)

Hook: TMC 100—size 16, 18, 20
Tying: Thread 8-0 black
Body: Tying thread with touch of superglue
Wingpost: Black Hi-Vis® fibers
Hackle: 1 grizzly, 1 brown, palmered full length

Tying and Fishing Notes: See Fore and Aft Midge, page 46.

Fore and Aft Midge

Hook: TMC 100—size 18, 20

Thread: Black 8-0

Tail: Black hackle fibers

Rear-hackle: Grizzly

Mid-body: Tying thread

Front hackle: Grizzly

Tying Notes: The previous three surface adults represent multiple individual insects, allowing larger hook sizes and better visibility. The superglue on the Griffith's Gnat ensures durability—a friend, on the Bighorn, took ten good fish on one fly. The Griffith's Gnat variations are simply palmered hackle over tying thread. One has a black wingpost for visibility. The Fore and Aft requires two small hackles separated by a tying thread body. It represents two midges.

Fishing Notes:

The effectiveness of these three flies goes beyond imitating groups of midges. The patterns are often used, with success, when only sporadic midge activity is present. These larger imitations are visible and float well over faster, choppy water. The black wingpost is easy to see when looking into water with a lot of reflected light. I often use Griffith's Gnats as attractors while "prospecting" smaller streams.

The Griffith's Gnat, like the Adams (page 90), is useful in so many situations that it qualifies as a "universal" dry fly. Notably, each of these flies has Michigan origins.

Blue-Winged Olives (BWO)

There are several mayflies matched by patterns called "Blue-Winged Olives": Baetis, Pseudocloeon, some Ephemerellas and Paraleptophlebias. The imitations presented here should cover most situations where you see naturals with gray-olive or brown-olive bodies and grayish wings. (See the Hatch Chart, page 94, for the various hatching periods.)

We have already discussed the nymphal stage of these insects: Olive Nymph (page 19), Small Olive Nymph (page 26), and Pheasant Tail (page 21). I'd like to present some effective film and surface patterns. I view these as YEAR-ROUND flies because the only month I haven't taken a midwestern trout on a BWO is January. My BWO fly box is in my right upper vest pocket through the season. The Baetis hatch is one of my favorite hatches, occurring on damp gray days, especially during spring and fall, although a cool, dark summer day will bring them out. When you see fish rising to "olives," look carefully at the surface to see what size is coming off. Preferring to fish on top, I'll usually tie on a dry pattern first, erring on the small side with respect to size—if they eat it, fine—if not, I'll switch to an emerger or floating nymph. Overall, I feel that the best midwestern olive patterns are the Olive Nymph and the BWO Parachute. For spinner patterns, see page 68.

Blue-Winged Olive Floating Nymph

Hook: TMC® 100—size 16, 18, 20

Thread: Olive 8-0

Tail: Wood duck flank

Abdomen: Olive beaver

Rib: Pearlescent Krystal Flash®

Thorax: Brown Australian opossum

Wingcase/wing: Gray cul-de-canard (CDC) fibrils

Tying Notes: This tie is similar to the Olive Nymph (page 19). Keep the abdomen thin. I use natural gray CDC feathers from wild birds collected during the duck season. The fibrils are stripped from the quill before tying in. They are tied in wingcase-style, then doubled back on top and trimmed one-third to one-half the way back over abdomen.

Fishing Notes:

During a midwestern olive hatch, I think trout eat more nymphs than adults. This is a good pattern to try if the trout are visibly active at the surface but not particularly interested in adult imitations. The imitation is fished upstream, or up and across like a dry fly. The CDC fibers allow reasonable visibility.

Blue-Winged Olive Wet-Dry

Hook: TMC® 100—size 16, 18 20

Tail: Wood duck flank

Body: Gray and olive beaver, 50-50

Rib: Pearlescent Krystal Flash®

Hackle: 1 turn of gray duck shoulder (covert) feather

Tying Notes: With a few minor variations (adding a short tail and ribbing), this is a very effective pattern taken from Gary Borger's book Nymphing. *The hackle fibers should be a bit longer than the body and extend back along the body like a soft hackle. The body is thin.*

Fishing Notes:

Borger notes that the covert hackle feathers are stiff enough to support the fly on the surface (dry fly) and yet supple enough to allow the fly to be pulled easily under (wet fly) if conditions demand. This fly represents either an emerger or a drowned adult and is another option to try if the trout are not taking the upright-winged adults. As the name implies, it is fished as either a dry or a wet fly. To fish it wet, simply pull it under the surface, let it drift and then swing in the current.

This pattern performs very well as a trailing fly behind a lightly weighted nymph or Cress Bug in slower currents, especially large back-eddies.

Blue-Winged Olive No-Hackle Emerger

Hook: TMC® 100—size 16, 18 20

Tail: Wood duck flank fibers

Body: Olive-gray beaver, mix

Rib: Pearlescent Krystal Flash®

Wing: Duck quill segments

Tying Notes: Same as the Wet-Dry except omit the hackle and tie a short segment of duck quill wing on each side (can substitute the tips of duck shoulder feather, gray "poly" or CDC tuft instead) about the length of the body or slightly less. Add a bit of dubbing in front of wing.

Fishing Notes:

The three flies just discussed, the Blue-Winged Olive Floating Nymph, Blue-Winged Olive Wet-Dry and the Blue-Winged Olive No-Hackle Emerger, fill the same need. They are to be used during a blue-winged olive hatch when the upright-winged adults are not particularly effective. Fishing these flies, as mentioned, may vary from a strictly dead drift dry fly presentation to a wet fly swing. A small amount of weight may be needed if you note trout feeding a foot or two beneath the surface.

The Castle Rock in southwestern Wisconsin is known for excellent blue-winged olive hatches (especially Baetis) and well-educated trout. This combination results in a blue-winged olive "clinic." There is one particular back-eddy where the trout can be easily observed. During an Olive hatch, you can see the trout moving here and there to intercept naturals. This situation allows you to work out an approach: getting in position for the best casting angle, planning where your line must land and where the fly needs to be. I usually try to fish to a particular trout, preferring to fish with a dry fly if possible. Often, however, the fish will take only an occasional upright-winged adult and feed mainly on nymphs and emergers. Now is the time to tie on one of the floating nymphs, wet-dries, or no-hackle emergers. At times, a small amount of weight and an indicator is needed. If this is the case, try to watch the trout instead of the indicator. If the fish moves a bit, wiggles its tail or opens its mouth—tighten. I won't forget a good-sized trout that took my fly—I didn't realize it at the time because I was watching the indicator, which never moved. I did see the fish eject my fly though— another trout fishing lesson.

Most of the time, you don't have the luxury of fishing to visible fish. All you see is the riseform. Goddard and Clarke, in their classic book *The Trout and the Fly*, offer an insightful study of riseforms that is well worth reading and which will help you make your decision on surface versus film presentations.

Blue-Winged Olive
Parachute ★

Hook: TMC® 100—size 14, 16, 18, 20; TMC 101—size 22, 24 (most used are sizes 18, 22)

Thread: Gray 8-0

Tail: Stiff high-quality blue dun hackle fibers

Abdomen: Gray and olive beaver, mix to approximate BCS 28

Wingpost: Gray, white or black turkey flats: May substitute small natural gray CDC feather from wood duck or mallard for gray wing, or black Hi-Vis® fibers for black wing

Hackle: High-quality blue dun

Thorax: Brown Australian opossum (BCS 35) on size 14—use same dubbing as abdomen on smaller sizes

Tying Notes: Parachutes are fairly easy to tie. Tie them by the dozens; you'll use them (making a few in darker shades, size 16, 18 for "Paraleps"). They float well and are surprisingly durable. This is my favorite dry fly pattern.

To tie, starting at the one-third length behind hook eye, tie in a width of turkey flat (see Figure 11) appropriate for hook size. The tips should be protruding well forward of hook eye; they will be trimmed later. Wrap back to secure the fibers, snip the butt and continue winding to the bend of the hook where a ball of thread (eight to nine wraps) is made to help splay the tail fibers.

Tie in hackle fiber tail (see A. K. Best's Production Fly Tying *on tailing). Use about 10-12 fibers on size 14; 8-10 fibers on size 16-20; 6-8 fibers on size 22, 24. The tail should be a bit long, and the fibers should splay horizontally. Use your thumbnail to splay if needed. Trim the tail fiber butts where they meet wingpost butt; apply wax to thread and a thin amount of dubbing. (I will often apply a bit of paste floatant with a toothpick to the shank before wrapping the dubbing.) Wrap the dubbing, very thinly in front of the tail then thicker around the wing butt. (If you use a rotary vise, it is easier to wind the dubbing with the hook in the upside-down position.) Grasp the forward protruding wingpost (hook now upright), hold it vertically and take a turn or two of dubbing in front of post to stand it up.*

Tie in the prepared hackle—hold it nearly vertical, shiny side toward you, with the short butt pointing downward on the near side of the hook, just in front of the wingpost. A short butt will not need to be trimmed. Apply a small amount of dubbing in front of wingpost and let the thread hang just behind the hook eye. Grasp the hackle tip with a hackle pliers and wind several turns around the post, which should be long enough to grasp and hold while winding the hackle.

After winding the hackle around the post, each turn below the previous turn, tie it off just behind the eye with three turns of thread, snip the hackle tip and secure the hackle with three or four wraps back while holding the forward-protruding hackle fibers out of the way. Whip finish, re-align the hackle fibers, snip the wingpost to proper length, shape, and the fly is complete.

If CDC is used for the wingpost, include the quill to help it stand up.

Fishing Notes:

In small sizes, this is a deadly Pseudocloeon pattern, thus useful in mid- and late summer. Springtime Paraleptophlebias are imitated in size 16 and 18 with a darker brown-olive body. The pattern is excellent for summertime Ephemerella "Olives" and for "year-round" Baetis. The spring and fall Baetis hatches are favorites of mine, occurring on damp, cloudy days on most of our upper midwestern streams. Look for little gray "sailboat" wings drifting down the currents—and rising trout.

I've had days when the trout preferred the imitation to the natural—when you could cast to the upper feeding area, let it drift, and know the fly wouldn't make it to the end of the drift without being taken. These situations make up for others that aren't quite as successful.

Use the patterns with the dark wingpost in situations where there is a lot of light reflected off the water. The white wingpost is highly visible if there is little reflected light. The CDC post matches the wing color of the dun almost exactly, and the fly is an excellent floater.

In exacting conditions, I'll use the fly described next—the Quill-Winged Olive. The Parachute Adams and traditional Adams (page 90) are also reasonable BWO imitations. One day after catching multiple trout on the BWO Parachute, I switched to a Parachute Adams and witnessed a mid-sized trout rise to the Adams, open its mouth but not close it on the fly. It simply backed away from the less exact imitation!

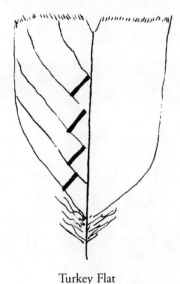

Turkey Flat

Figure 11:

The wingpost for the BWO Parachute and others is a snip (heavy black line) from the turkey flat. The turkey flat fibers are then tied to the shank as drawn. Fibers are left long for easy handling when winding the hackle. Following the tie-in of post, the thread is taken to bend of hook, a slight ball of thread is made; then tailing hackle fibers are tied just in front of ball to splay them.

Quill-Winged Olive

Hook: TMC® 100—size 16, 18, 20

Tail: Stiff blue dun hackle fibers

Abdomen: Olive-gray beaver

Wing: Paired duck quills; can substitute gray hackle tips

Thorax: Brown Australian opossum on size 16—
olive-gray beaver on size 18, 20

Hackle: Blue dun

Tying Notes: I like to have the wings slanting backward a bit over the body but not quite 45 degrees. A blue dun hackle is tied in front of the wing, the thorax dubbed, then the hackle is wound forward over the dubbing. It may be trimmed on the bottom if desired.

Fishing Notes:

See BWO Parachute, page 50.

SEASONAL FLIES

SEASONAL flies need to be carried during their times of emergence, given in the text and the Hatch Chart (page 94).

Mayflies

Mayflies are classic "trout insects." The greatest share of the life of the mayfly is spent as the nymph beneath the surface. During the time of emergence, which is usually quite well-defined for each species, the nymphs rise to the surface (usually) and molt or emerge into the adult form, the upright-winged dun. The duns leave the surface and within the span of minutes to a day or two, molt again into the reproductive phase, the spinner. The spinners mate in the air over the stream, then fall spent to the surface where the females lay their eggs. The entire life span of the adult is only a few hours to days. Certain stages of a particular species may be more important to the trout (and the angler) than other stages. For example, the spinner of the Gray Drake is very important, while the dun assumes very little importance.

Fishing the Au Sable.

Mayflies
Hendrickson

The "Hendrickson" is the female dun version of Ephemerella subvaria, a size 14 mayfly which hatches throughout the upper Midwest from mid April through May, dwindling in June. The male dun imitation is called the Red Quill. Hendricksons hatch during the day, but hatching days can be quite unpredictable. The spinners fall in the evenings. The trout look for these flies early in the season—so should you; hitting the hatch right can be an awesome experience.

Hendrickson Parachute

Hook: TMC® 100—size 14

Thread: Gray 8-0

Tail: Stiff, high-quality blue dun hackle fibers, split

Body: Beaver, mixed to approximate BCS 121—I use Mad River® Pink Fox

Wingpost: Gray turkey flat

Hackle: Ginger

Red Quill

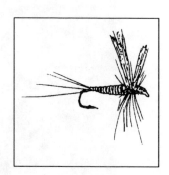

Hook: TMC 100—size 14

Thread: Gray 8-0

Tail: Blue dun hackle fibers

Body: Red-brown hackle quill, soaked (can substitute red-brown dubbing)

Wing: Wood duck flank fibers, split

Hackle: Blue dun

Hendrickson
Duck-Shoulder Dun—DSD

Hook: TMC 100—size 14

Thread: Gray 8-0

Tail: Blue dun hackle fibers

Body: Same as Hendrickson Parachute

Wing: Duck shoulder covert feathers

Legs: Wood duck flank fibers

Head: Dubbing

Tying Notes: The Hendrickson Parachute is tied as described for the BWO Parachute (page 50). (Tie a couple in size 12, dark brown, in case you run into the Black Quill in your area.) The Red Quill is a traditional Catskill dry fly. For the DSD, prepare suitably sized covert feathers by snipping the fibers from each side of the base of the quill, leaving enough fibers at the tip to simulate the partly emerged wing. Tie one on each side, slanting back, concave side out. Add a few wood duck fibers on each side for legs and dub a small thorax-head in front.

Fishing Notes:

The best Hendrickson hatch I've seen occurred on the Mecan River in late April, 1992—seven days before Wisconsin's general season opener. All we could do was sit and watch—and learn—and design a few flies. The Hendrickson hatch is widespread in midwestern streams, from the Black Earth to the Brule. During the hatch, the nymph (dark hare's ear, size 14), fished in the morning, swinging at the end of the drift can be effective. During the emergence, try to select a good riser; use a fairly long tippet, 5X or 6X, and generally use the low-floating parachute or DSD. The fully hackled pattern is useful on choppier water. If you are not doing as well as you'd like, look closely to make sure the trout aren't feeding on smaller mayflies such as the Blue Quill (Paraleptophlebia adoptiva) in which case, you'll need a size 16 or 18 BWO Parachute or a small Adams (page 90). The Little Black Caddis also hatches at the same time as the Hendrickson.

The spinner pattern is a size 14-16 rusty spinner, discussed later (page 68).

Sulphurs

The sulphurs are light yellow, size 16 (Ephemerella invaria) and size 18 (Ephemerella dorothea) mayflies that start hatching in mid-May and continue through June, with some sporadic lingering activity as the season progresses. This is a very important hatch throughout the upper Midwest and occurs on virtually all streams. The hatch usually begins in early evenings but can begin in the afternoon on gray days. The nymphs and "emergers" have already been discussed (page 21)—use a size 16-18 Pheasant Tail Nymph sub-surface and a Pheasant Tail Soft-Hackle in the film. (For spinners, see page 68.)

Sulphur Sparkle Dun

Hook: TMC® 100—size 16, 18; TMC 102Y—size 17

Thread: Yellow 8-0

Shuck: Olive Zelon®, same length as body

Abdomen: Yellow-orange dubbing to approximate BCS 53—
  Hareline® fur dubbing #15 or SLF® finesse are good choices

Wing: Coastal deer hair, tied Compara-dun style

Tying Notes: Excellent instructions for tying Compara-duns and Sparkle Duns are given in Randall Kaufmann's book Tying Dry Flies. *Also see Skip Morris' book* The Art of Tying the Dry Fly.

Fishing Notes:

The value of the Sulphur Sparkle Dun became apparent to me fishing with two pros of the Wolf River, Wayne Anderson and George Close, who demonstrated that with proper presentation, the fly is nearly "automatic" with trout rising to sulphurs. George says, "With the Sparkle Dun, you've got the fly you need; all you need to do is present it properly." George uses a 4X tippet on the Wolf River in anticipation of large fish, especially at dark. He relies on casting skill for short, "accurate" drifts allowing the trout to see the fly first. On smaller spring creeks, a 5X or 6X tippet is my choice.

COLORPLATE 9
—— MAYFLIES ——

Hexagenia Parachute
p. 62

Hexagenia Spinner
p. 64

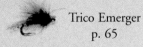

Trico Emerger
p. 65

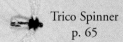

Trico Spinner
p. 65

White Mayfly
p. 67

White Mayfly Parachute
p. 67

A beautiful winter-caught rainbow that took a size 20 Pheasant Tail.

Spring Coulee, a spring creek gem of southwestern Wisconsin that supports excellent Blue-Winged Olive hatches.

COLORPLATE 11

—— MAYFLY SPINNERS ——

Close Carpet Fly Spinner
p. 68

Hendrickson Spinner
p. 68

Blue-Winged Olive Spinner
p. 68

Sulphur Spinner
p. 68

Tiny Yellow
p. 68

Little Yellow Stonefly
p. 69

Calf Hair Downing
p. 69

Partridge and Yellow Soft-Hackle
p. 70

Central Wisconsin's Mecan River in Waushara County.
It is one of many excellent "sand county" streams. The Mecan is noted
for its Hexagenia hatch.

Sulphur CDC Parachute ★

Hook: TMC® 100—size 16, 18; TMC 102Y—size 17

Thread: Yellow 8-0

Tail: Ginger hackle fibers

Body: Beaver, yellow to match BCS 42, 46

Wingpost: Natural gray CDC feather, quill included—
can substitute white turkey flat

Hackle: Ginger

Tying Notes: Tie as noted for BWO Parachute (page 50).

Fishing Notes:

When the sulphur hatch begins in the evening, the smaller trout begin rising first. Use these smaller fish for practice—trying curve casts, slack line casts, long and short casts and practicing loop control. As evening progresses, larger fish begin to rise and you will be ready for them. I generally use 5X tippet. If visibility becomes difficult, use the White Wing Post Parachute (Turkey Flat) and use a crisp straight-line cast—you'll know your fly is straight off the end of your fly line and you can strike if you see a rise in that vicinity. The CDC Parachute has been an excellent pattern for me. Sometimes it is difficult to tell the difference between the fly and the naturals on the water.

Brown Drake, March Brown, Gray Fox, Isonychia sp.

These flies are listed together because the imitations are quite similar; even the Isonychia can be included. The Brown Drake (Ephemera simulans) is a size 10 tan-brown mayfly with dark brown blotches on the wing. The March Brown (Stenonema vicarium) is a size 12 and brown, while the Gray Fox (Stenonema fuscum) is size 12 (or a bit smaller) and tan-gray. Isonychia are size 10-12 and "mahogany" in color. The Brown Drakes hatch over a brief period the first couple of weeks in June, just before dark—this can be a very important hatch. The Stenonemas hatch from mid-May through mid-June in the afternoons and evenings and are of varying importance. I've seen into Isonychia as late as August (see the Hatch Chart, page 94, for approximate emergence periods of these insects).

The following two patterns should cover you for these large mayflies. Carry several size 10 and 12 and a few size 14 dark to light brown imitations during this hatching period.

Adams Hair-Wing

Hook: TMC® 2312—size 10, 12, 14

Thread: Black or brown 6-0

Tail/abdomen: Deer body hair

Rib: Tying thread

Wing: Deer body hair, divided

Hackle: "Adams hackle"—1 grizzly, 1 brown

Tying Notes: This pattern is the famous "Cap's Hair-Wing" or the "Ed Haaga Fly" of Wisconsin's Wolf River, originally tied by Ed Haaga in the late 1960's for Cap Buettner's fly shop. The "Adams Hair-Wing" is a bit of a misnomer because the only feature in common with the Adams is the hackle. The pattern works for many larger mayflies, as previously noted, and is also used by some fly fishers for the Gray Drake, discussed later (page 60). To tie, wrap the shank in the area of the abdomen with tying thread and coat with head cement. Snip off a small "pencil" of deer hair from the hide and cut to the combined length of tail and body (the body being the forward extension of the tail ribbed with tying thread). Use dark-colored hair for darker bodies, light for lighter bodies. Tie in hair by the butt, on top of the shank, starting about one-third length behind the hook eye. Wrap thread backward firmly in medium spirals down to the tail area and then forward to the original tie-in area. The front one-third of the shank is bare. The tail should not flare appreciably, and the body should be bound by "x" wraps of thread. Tie in another bunch of deer hair, stacked Compara-dun style for the wing; stand it upright and divide it. Trim wing butts where they butt against abdomen. Tie in hackles behind wing, wind a few turns of hackle behind wing and a few in front; then tie off.

Fishing Notes:

See Close Carpet Fly.

Close Carpet Fly

Hook: TMC® 2312—size 10, 12, 14

Thread: Black 6-0

Tail/abdomen: Deer body hair

Wing: Deer hair, Compara-dun style

Thorax: Coarse Antron® fibers from carpet sample,
gray-tan-brown

Tying Notes: This fly was designed by George Close of Kiel, Wisconsin, at the time Antron was becoming popular as a fly tying material. George desired a more flush-floating pattern than the Adams Hair-Wing for some situations. The carpet Antron was selected because its coarseness applied to large-sized imitations. The tail, abdomen and wing are tied as in the Adams Hair-Wing, except the wing is not divided. A dubbing loop is formed for the Antron fibers, which are cut from a "loop" of the carpet (the fibers are about one-half to three-quarters-inch long). The fibers are arranged in the loop, trimmed if needed, spun and wound tightly one or two turns behind the wing, two or three turns ahead of wing and tied off. The Antron is trimmed on the bottom to half the width of hook gap, and the wing is spread Compara-dun style.

A few variations of the Close Carpet Fly and Adams Hair-Wing may be tried: varying the thread color or applying thin dubbing to the abdomen to more accurately match the color of the natural; using white calf tail wings on the Adams Hair-Wing for increased nighttime visibility; substituting snowshoe hare's foot fibers for the Antron in the Close Carpet Fly.

Fishing Notes:

If you hit it right, the Brown Drake hatch can be very impressive. Brown Drake nymphs prefer streams with sand-gravel bottoms and during the hatching period ascend to the surface with undulating movements. The Marabou-Tailed Hare's Ear Nymph (page 25) should be twitched to mimic this behavior. Emergence occurs under low light conditions—the dun emerges on the surface—an event which is well-noticed by the trout as evidenced by their obvious rises. Either the Adams Hair-Wing or the Close Carpet Fly may be used when the fish are feeding on the duns. Spinners fall a day or two later, in the evening, and are steadily sipped by the fish well into the night. A spinner pattern is mandatory at this time— even if you can't see it. I've spent a few frustrating nights discovering that the fully hackled pattern is not what the trout want. They want a flush, spent wing imitation. The Close Carpet Fly, with wings split to 180 degrees and secured with a drop of head cement between them, will do the job—fished in medium to slow water.

The Stenonema and Isonychia "events" are variable. It is a good idea to have a few size 10, 12, and 14 Adams Hair-Wings or Close Carpet Flies with you to cover situations where you encounter trout rising to these larger mayflies.

Gray Drake

This size 12 gray mayfly (Siphlonurus sp.) is very important on larger midwestern streams with stretches of fast water. It is a premier hatch on Michigan's Pere Marquette and Wisconsin's Wolf—emerging from late May through June. The important stage is the spinner.

Gray Drake Parachute

Hook: TMC® 2312—size 12

Thread: Black 6-0

Tail: Moose hair

Body: Gray muskrat

Rib: Tying thread

Wingpost: White turkey flat

Hackle: Blue dun or grizzly (multiple wraps around post for floatability)

Tying Notes: Standard parachute tie (see BWO Parachute, page 50). Use eight or nine moose hairs, slightly split for the tail. The body should be very thin and ribbed with the tag end of the tying thread.

Fishing Notes:

I had fished this hatch for several years but really didn't know much about the insect. Dick Pobst, of Thornapple Orvis shop in Ada, Michigan, provided me much essential information on the naturals and how to fish them. The naturals have a very thin light gray abdomen, ribbed dark gray. They appear by the thousands—suddenly—at dusk, bringing up fish "all over the place." The spinners fall over the riffles and are washed to the quieter water down-current. I find the Gray Drake Parachute very effective as a spinner pattern. This is a night-time event, and the wingpost is visible in the riffles as well as the quieter water down-current. It has produced well for me. Use 3X or 4X tippet and be prepared to hook large fish—then chase after them in heavy water after dark. They can take you to places you really don't want to go!

Light Cahill

The Light Cahill (Stenocron canadense) is a light yellow, size 14 mayfly that appears from early to mid-June and tapers through July. (A similar smaller insect may appear in late July and August—use a size 16 sulphur imitation for this.) It is often seen by fly fishers who have arrived a few days early for the Hex hatch or in the hours preceding Hex activity. Take a few Light Cahills with you—the pattern is simply a Sulphur CDC Parachute (page 57) tied on a size 14 hook.

Light Cahill Parachute

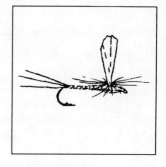

Hook: TMC® 100—size 14

Thread: Light yellow 8-0

Tail: Ginger hackle fibers, split

Body: Light yellow beaver

Wing post: Light gray turkey flat

Hackle: Ginger

Tying Notes: See tying instructions for Blue-Winged Olive Parachute (page 50).

Fishing Notes:

Seeing Light Cahills is always pleasant. They are easy to identify and the trout respond to them. Emergence is often in the evening, earlier on gray days. A duck-shoulder dun emerger (like Hendrickson DSD but light yellow) may be useful. At times during Hexagenia activity, the Light Cahill Parachute may take fish when the huge Hex imitations are not producing.

Hexagenia Limbata

This is the famous giant mayfly—size 6 and 8 with a creamy yellow abdomen and darker thorax. The Hex emerges throughout the Midwest starting about the second week of June in the southern and central areas with emergence progressing to late June and tapering through mid-July in northern areas. Sporadic activity may occur weeks after the "main" hatch. The emergence of duns and the spinner falls starts at dusk and continues into the night. The sheer numbers of the huge insects can be incredible, as is the response of the trout. All phases of the Hex—nymph (page 27), dun and spinner—are important.

Hexagenia Parachute ★

Hook: TMC® 2302—size 6, 8

Thread: Yellow 6-0

Tail: "V" hackle fibers

Extended body: Glo-Bug® yarn (Oregon cheese)

Body: Yellow foam covered with light yellow rabbit dubbing

Wingpost: White calf body hair, long,

Hackle: 1 grizzly, 1 brown wrapped around post

Thorax: Light yellow rabbit dubbing

Tying Notes: First, pre-assemble a couple dozen tail/extended body units (see Figure 12). This is done by cutting Glo-Bug yarn into one and one-half to two-inch sections and dividing each section into three strands. Fashion the "V"-shaped tails from large brown neck hackle fibers.

Insert the bare quill into the Glo-Bug segment and superglue (Permabond® 102 works very well).

To construct the fly, simply lash the tail/body unit to the hook, leaving a suitable amount of extension. Tie in a small segment of yellow closed-cell foam over the yarn and dub the abdomen with yellow rabbit.

Tie in the wingpost, stand it up, tie in hackles (hackle fibers should be fairly long), dub the thorax and wind the hackles. The foam ensures floatation. The extended body of yarn is non-rigid, permitting hookability better than a rigid body extension. The fly can also be tied as a divided hair-wing with conventional hackling.

There are hundreds of effective Hex imitations. Vern Lunde, of Lunde's Fly Fishing Chalet in Mt. Horeb, Wisconsin, told me he sold out of his regular Hex ties on one occasion, but customers were buying his large Royal Wulffs and humpies—the customers returned later, related their success, and bought more of the same.

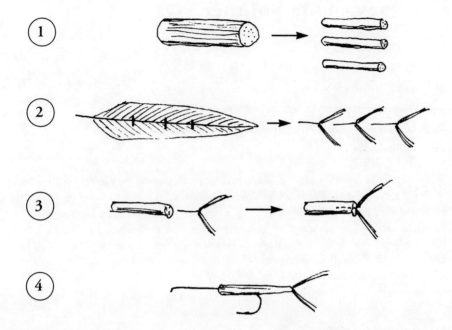

Figure 12:

1. A two-inch section is cut from a rope of Glo-Bug Yarn. It is divided parallel to the fibers into three smaller sections.
2. Tail fiber "V" is snipped and stripped from large hackle feathers. Treat the fiber-quill "V" junction with head cement.
3. Insert the quill into the yarn segment and glue with Permabond® 102.
4. Tie assembly onto hook. For the White Mayfly (page 67), use white poly yarn.

Fishing Notes:

See Hexagenia Spinner, page 64.

Hexagenia Spinner

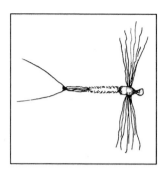

Hook: TMC® 2302—size 6-8

Thread: Yellow 6-0

Tail/extended body: Same as Hex Parachute

Body: Yellow foam covered with light yellow rabbit dubbing

Wing: White bucktail mixed with Flashabou®

Thorax: Yellow foam

Tying Notes: The extended tail and abdomen are tied the same as the Hexagenia Parachute. A strip of yellow closed-cell foam about three-sixteenths-inch wide is then tied in, just ahead of the abdomen (like the first step of tying in a wingcase). This foam will later be pulled over "wingcase-style" to hold the wings in "spinner position." Tie in the bucktail wing with tips extending back over the body. Add a small amount of dubbing over the tied-in butts of the wing and foam. Then divide and spread the bucktail to "spinner wing" position, pull the foam over the spread and divided wing and tie off.

Fishing Notes:

First prepare yourself for nighttime fishing for large fish in brushy streams with mosquitoes. Get to the stream early enough to memorize your way out; take a fairly substantial rod, and remember to take insect repellent and a light. If you wear glasses, take your clear ones if you're starting out with Polaroids. On the stream, select a "beat" and figure out your casting lanes if trees and brush are factors. I like to figure out a backcast lane and project it forward to a landmark ahead of me—so that I can line up my backcast with my forward landmark.

The insects don't appear until dark—when the whippoorwills and barred owls begin to call and the bats appear. Sometimes you are able to fish a Brown Drake (page 58) or Cahill Spinner fall before the Hexes appear. When they do appear, you will want to use a short leader with 2X or 3X tippet. Avoid tangles at night. Usually the smaller fish start feeding first—when the large fish begin, you will know. Often the best trout feed immediately in front of snags (the reason for 2X and stout rods).

The fully hackled patterns are easier to see, but if spinners are on the water, a flush floating imitation is mandatory. Consider a Hex Nymph (page 27) or a Light Cahill Parachute (page 61) if the fish begin to ignore your surface Hex pattern.

Rivers especially famous for their Hex hatch include Michigan's Au Sable and northern Wisconsin's White River system.

Hitting the Hex hatch right is one of the most memorable of fly-fishing events and is a great generator of fly-fishing lore, like the night my friend, Dick Ward, hooked a good fish on his backcast. Hitting the hatch wrong is a common experience. Getting off the stream at 10:30 p.m. with a one hour drive ahead of you, not having seen one Hex, especially if it happens a couple of nights in a row, can wear you down. But the thing of it is, you really don't want to miss hitting this hatch right.

Tricorythodes

When you start seeing these tiny black (size 22, 24) mayflies in July, you know you're in for challenging fly-fishing. The hatch lasts into October and provides consistent morning activity: Early morning in July, late morning in early fall. The spinner is the important pattern—nymphs and emergers are also very useful.

Trico Emerger

Hook: Daiichi® 1140—size 20, 22

Thread: Black 8-0

Tail: Wood duck flank

Abdomen: Olive beaver

Wing: Gray muskrat

Thorax: Black beaver or mole

Trico Spinner ★

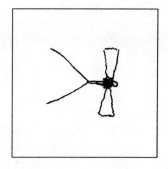

Hook: TMC® 101—size 22, 24

Thread: Black or tan 8-0

Tail: Blue dun hackle fibers, tied long and split

Abdomen: Tying thread

Wing: Twinkle organza (fly shop or fabric store)

Thorax: Beaver or mole

Tying Notes: The emerger is a straightforward tie. Make sure to tie the tail short and dub the thin abdomen well down on the bend of the hook. The emerging wing is a short tuft of muskrat projecting back over the abdomen. The thorax is dubbed as a pronounced "dot" in front of the wing.

For the spinner, tie in the tail first using about eight stiff, high-quality hackle fibers, splitting the fibers with the aid of a small ball of tying thread (see A. K. Best's book Production Fly Tying, *section on tailing). Wind a thin abdomen. For wing, use twinkle organza fibers separated from the fabric and long enough to handle easily. "Figure of eight" the fibers to the shank, a short distance behind hook eye and criss-cross thorax dubbing over and around the wing to create a pronounced "dot" and tie off. Trim the wings to proper length.*

Tie dozens of these. They are not difficult to tie and you will need them. The organza is the best material I've found for the wing, by far—a tip from Gary Borger. This fly is durable and it works—not only in the Midwest but on all good Trico water.

Fishing Notes:

I always look forward to seeing the clouds of Trico spinners over the riffles in the morning—it means good fishing on the quieter water below. Use a long lightweight rod for larger water—a shorter rod for smaller water with long leaders and 7X or 8X tippet. Tricos in the Midwest will bring up respectable trout, and in heavily fished streams, such as Wisconsin's Willow and Kinnickinnic in St. Croix County, they become extremely discriminating—leaving very little margin for error. Get as close to the risers as possible, trying to place your fly a few inches above the fish. Casting from the side or down to the fish will keep your leader away from them. The tippet should fall loosely to avoid drag. At times, if visibility is a problem, I'll use either a small foam indicator or a small Parachute Adams (page 90) as an indicator fly. If you meet with rejection, tie the Small Black Nymph (page 26) or the Trico Emerger behind the indicator fly.

Fishing Tricos is an excellent way to improve your skills. The hatch occurs nearly daily on many of our midwestern streams, giving the fly fisher ample opportunity for practice. Be sure to look for Tricos—check the streamside cobwebs, the back eddies and look for clouds of insects where the swallows and waxwings are active.

Ephoron leukon (White Mayfly)

The White Mayfly is a size 12 to 14 mayfly with a white body and light gray wing, appearing about the second week of August and lasting into September. The hatches occur in the evening and are especially good on midwestern streams with a bed of gravel and rock. Hatching is very obvious, starting gradually in early evening and building strongly over the next hour or two. The hatch brings up good numbers of trout that are not too particular about either pattern or presentation—an enjoyable situation.

White Mayfly ★

Hook: TMC® 100—size 12, 14

Thread: Gray 6-0, 8-0

Tail/extended abdomen: Shuck of white poly yarn with "V" white tail fibers (a tail assembly like the Hexagenia patterns, Figure 12)

Body: SLF finesse, white, or white rabbit

Wing: Calf body hair

Hackle: White

Tying Notes: Tie in calf body hair-wing fibers, leaving them extending forward over hook eye. Trim the wing butts. Next, lash the tail/extended body to shank, leaving a suitable amount of extension behind the bend of the hook. Dub the abdomen, stand up, and divide wing. Tie in hackle, add dubbing in front of wing, wind hackle, a few turns behind and a few turns ahead of the wing, and tie off. This pattern is effective. It can be varied by tying as a parachute if you desire a flush floating imitation or as an emerger with short gray wings slanted back over abdomen (DSD style), hackle trimmed on the bottom.

Fishing Notes:

I usually fish the Ephoron leukon hatch on central Wisconsin's Tomorrow River (see Colorplate 6). It is always a pleasant surprise to see all the trout making a re-appearance "on top," something they hadn't done during the heat of July.

Incredible numbers of insects come off in various stages of emergence. Duns will be flying around with trailing nymphal shucks still attached. Partly emerged adults drift on the surface with wings still trapped in the shuck, and spinners are swarming over the riffles. The fish are not particular—they seem to want to eat one insect and get on to the next one. The feeding period lasts a few hours, from early evening, then dwindles after dark. The Ephoron hatch will bring up large trout, especially late in the evening. Generally, a four-weight rod with 4X tippet is adequate.

This hatch is excellent for the beginning fly fisher.

Mayfly Spinners

Spinners represent the final phase in the life of the mayfly. The duns transform to the reproductive phase, developing clear wings and usually thinner and darker bodies.

Spinners need to be considered anytime you see mayflies. For most mayflies, when you see the duns, the spinners will be close behind. Generally, spinner activity is in the evening or periods of low light. Morning spinner falls occur as well—Tricos being a good example. Female spinners are attracted to riffles to lay their eggs; they fall along with the males and are carried down-current. Massive concentrations of spinners can form in eddies and current channels. Trout love to sip spinners on the surface, but sub-surface spinners can be important. Some Baetis (Blue-Winged Olive) spinners crawl beneath the surface to deposit their eggs and become available in the depths. I've seen trout stuffed with fresh Trico spinners that were swept under by currents and taken there by trout which hadn't been rising.

Spinner imitations are needed in sizes 6 through 24. Tie the abdomens thin with a bulge at the thorax. Wings are tied at 180 degrees, flat to the surface and tails are split. Some standard dry fly patterns, the Compara-duns and parachutes, work very well as spinners and allow good visibility.

The following chart supplies a summary of spinners. Carry them as you would the dun patterns.

MAYFLY SPINNERS CHART

INSECT	DRY FLY HOOK SIZE	TAIL	BODY	WING	NOTES
BLUE-WINGED OLIVE	14-22	Dun hackle fibers	Olive-brown	Twinkle organza	
HENDRICKSON	14	Moose	Rust	Dun hackle tips	
SULPHURS	16-18	Dun hackle fibers	Yellow abdomen rusty thorax	Twinkle organza	
BROWN DRAKE STENONEMA SP. ISONYCHIA SP.	10 12 10, 12				Use Close Carpet Fly with wings divided to180° and tail split
GRAY DRAKE	12, 14				Use parachute pattern, see text (page 60)
LIGHT CAHILL	14				Use size 14 "Sulphur" Spinner
HEXAGENIA LIMBATA	6, 8				See text (page 64)
TRICORYTHODES	22, 24				See text (page 65)
WHITE MAYFLY	12, 14				Use parachute pattern (page 67)
TINY YELLOW SPINNER	22, 24	Dun hackle fibers	Yellow	Twinkle organza	Good for tiny light-colored spinners occasionally encountered

Stoneflies

The flat down-winged stonefly adults are of importance to the midwestern fly fisher. Small dark brown and black adults occur on some of our faster streams during late winter. Very large black to yellow-brown adults can be of importance at night during June and July. A few size 14 and 16 dark adult patterns and a few size 8 and 10 **Stimulators** in brown will do when you encounter these situations.

The most consistent stonefly adult action is provided by the Little Yellow Stonefly, which appears on the southern-most streams of the upper Midwest as early as late May and continues through the summer. Although these flies appear in small numbers, they are reasonably common; and trout, judging by their splashy riseforms, seem to relish them.

Little Yellow Stonefly

Hook: TMC® 100—size 14

Thread: Yellow 8-0

Tail: Elk hock bleached

Body: SLF finesse, yellow (BCS 47)

Wing: Mallard flank fibers with twinkle organza

Hackle: Dun

Tying Tips: The Little Yellow Stonefly is easy and fun to tie. Tie in a short tail, form a dubbing loop for the SLF, and then dub the body forward. The wing is tied down over the abdomen, extending to the tip of the tail. Tie in hackle and wrap in front of wing. The elk hock tail contributes to excellent floatation. Carry a half dozen with you in a fly box compartment throughout the summer.

By substituting a white calf body hair-wing, you can create an excellent nighttime down-wing attractor that probably represents a moth.

Fishing Notes:

The Little Yellow Stonefly imitation is a good choice on summer days or evenings if you feel like fishing on top, yet no surface activity is apparent. I usually think about stoneflies when they show up at my lantern at night while I am camping on the Wolf or Timber Coulee.

One evening in early August, the calf hair version resulted in two brown trout on two successive casts on Wisconsin's Little Green River (one 15-inch; one 16-inch).

Yellow Cranefly

The Yellow Craneflies have legs much longer and bodies much thinner than the Yellow Stonefly. The wings are thin and lacy. The insects flit along the surface in the evening resembling caddis—trout respond well to them. Emergence begins in May and continues through much of the summer. The Partridge and Yellow is a useful imitation. Keep a few of these with your stonefly imitations.

Partridge and Yellow Soft-Hackle

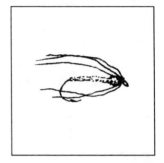

Hook: TMC® 100—size 14

Thread: Yellow 8-0

Body: SLF finesse, yellow—tied very thin with stray fibers clipped close

Hackle: Gray partridge or mallard flank—very long—at least one and one-half length of body

Tying Notes: This fly is extremely easy to tie. Dub a thin body; then take one turn of long soft hackle or simply strip a few fibers from the quill and tie in just behind the hook eye.

Fishing Notes:

As mentioned, craneflies "dance" above the surface in the evenings, looking much like caddis. Stomach contents of trout taken at this time may show surprising numbers of Yellow Craneflies. I generally fish the pattern upstream, dead drift, like a dry fly. It also works well swinging downstream, with action. The cranefly larvae resemble maggots and can create heavy feeding in local areas—a Tan Caddis Larva (page 32), fished deeply, will work in this situation.

Caddisflies

Matching caddisflies and fishing the imitations is more challenging than the mayflies for a variety of reasons. Caddisflies have more stages of development in their life cycle; their hatching periods generally are not as defined; and they exhibit various kinds of behavior.

Developing a fly box for caddis is definitely a learning experience. Caddis larval imitations have been discussed (page 32). Patterns for pupae, emergers and adults (including egg-laying and spent) will be presented here. These imitations represent some of the caddis common in the upper Midwest. On many occasions, classic patterns such as the Elk Hair and Fluttering Caddis in light and dark tones, along with the Henryville, sizes 14-20, are all that are necessary. On other occasions, not only the pattern but also the behavior must be exact. When the standard imitations are meeting with refusals, it's time to do some research and development—collect naturals and examine pumped stomach contents; then work out ties to match the caddis on the streams you fish. These ties will have important key features for each caddis phase, regardless of species:

Pupae are tied on curved hooks, TMC® 2487 or equivalent, with bodies of a translucent material like dubbed SLF. Ventral wings are usually fairly dark and "adherent" to the body—a tuft of muskrat or duck quill is a good choice. Trailing soft-hackle fibers represent legs and antennae. The head is dubbed fur or SLF.

Emergers are also tied on the TMC 2487, with a trailing shuck of Zelon® or poly yarn fibers, bodies of SLF (emerger and pupae bodies are usually a bit larger than the adult) and short dorsal "emerging" wings—poly yarn or snowshoe hare's foot fibers are excellent. The legs, antennae and head are similar to the pupa.

Adults have a body of fur/synthetic. For tent wings, raffia (Swiss straw), duck quill (gray) or natural turkey flats (tan-brown) are used. Coat the feathers with Flexament®. Other wing materials abound: poly yarn, CDC, hackle tips or fibers, elk and deer hair or synthetic films. Hackling can be varied from fully palmered to none. Standard dry fly hooks are used.

Spent adults and adults are tied on the same kind of hooks. Bodies are also the same. For wings, use hackle tips, raffia, duck shoulder or partridge body feathers—all tied spent. Hackling is minimal.

The *diving egg-laying adult* is tied the same as the adult with an underwing of twinkle organza to simulate trapped air.

My most-used caddis imitations are larvae, pupae and standard adults. Generally, most midwestern caddis fall in the 14-20 size range. On occasion, very large patterns are needed. I carry a few Stimulators, size 8-10, in brown/orange to mimic large caddis (and large stoneflies). Large, heavily hackled Elk Hairs are good on heavy water. I also carry a few "micro" caddis in black and tan, size 22.

The following patterns represent examples of caddis important in the upper Midwest: The Little Black Caddis (Chimarra sp.), the American Grannom (Brachycentrus sp.), the Tan Caddis (Hydropsyche sp.) and the Little Summer Green Caddis (Cheumatopsyche sp.). I would like to credit Carl Richards for insights on tying and fishing caddis patterns and would like to recommend two books soon to be published: one on caddis superhatches by Carl Richards and Dick Pobst; the other by Carl Richards and Bob Braendle, which will contain, among other things, keys to identifying caddis in our area.

Little Black Caddis Pupa

Hook: TMC® 2387—size 16, 18

Thread: Olive 8-0

Abdomen: Dark olive SLF finesse

Wing: Slate gray muskrat

Legs/antennae: Gray partridge fibers

Thorax/head: Black mole

Tying Notes: This imitation was tied as a result of stomach samplings of multiple trout during the emergence of the Little Black Caddis. The SLF abdomen is applied with a dubbing loop. Be sure to start well down on the bend of the hook. The tuft of muskrat fur is tied ventrally, like a beard. Legs/antennae are also ventral and fairly long. The pupae have the appearance of being covered with a film of mucous—a look that can be mimicked by enveloping the abdomen with clear raffia (Swiss straw), moistened before tying in. The wing/legs/antennae can also be tied by using a dubbing loop with muskrat fur, including guard hairs, wound in front of the abdomen, then trimming the top half to the shape of a thorax and head.

Fishing Notes:

See Little Black Caddis Adult, page 74.

COLORPLATE 13

—— CADDIS PATTERNS ——

Elk-Hair Caddis
p. 71

Fluttering Caddis
p. 71

Henryville
p. 71

Pupa
p. 72

Emerger
p. 73

Adult
(Raffia Wing)
p. 74

Adult
(Quill Wing)
p. 74

LITTLE BLACK CADDIS

Emerger

Adult

Spent

Little Summer
Green Caddis
p. 78

GRANNOM p. 75

Adult

Spent
(Hackle-Wing)

Pupa

Spent
(Raffia Wing)

TAN CADDIS p. 77

Stimulator
p. 69, 71

John Shillinglaw is about to land a 24-inch brown trout that took a size 16 Cress Bug fished through a channel in the "weed."

Photo—Tom Wendelburg

This 22-inch brown trout took a Wendelburg Cricket pattern on the west fork of the Kickapoo River.

COLORPLATE 15

—— TERRESTRIALS ——

June Bug
p. 80

BHP Beetle
p. 81

Clipped-Hackle Beetle
p. 82

Black Fur Ant
p. 83

Cinnamon Fur Ant
p. 84

Fall Flying Ant
p. 85

Cricket
p. 87

Hackle-Wing Hopper
p. 88

Inchworm
p. 86

—— SPECIAL FLIES AND ATTRACTORS ——

Adams
p. 90

Parachute Adams
p. 90

Pass Lake Dry
p. 91

Hornberg
p. 92

Royal Wulff
p. 93

*Fishing the structures
and riffles of a limestone
spring creek. There is an
abundance of these creeks in
the unglaciated "driftless"
terrain of northeast Iowa,
southeast Minnesota and
southwest Wisconsin.*

A native brown trout from Timber Coulee.

Little Black Caddis Emerger

Hook: TMC® 2387—size 16-18

Thread: Black 8-0

Shuck: Tan-gray poly yarn, to approximate BCS 91

Abdomen: Black SLF finesse—can add a bit of brown or olive beaver

Wing: Black or dark gray poly yarn

Legs/antennae: Gray partridge fibers

Head: Black mole

Tying Notes: This tie is similar to the pupa with the addition of a shuck and a dorsal wing. The curved hook allows the shuck to submerge. A touch of floatant to the wing will allow the imitation to assume a natural position in the film.

Fishing Notes:

See Little Black Caddis Adult, page 74.

Little Black Caddis Adult ★

Hook: TMC® 102Y—size 17, 19; TMC 100—size 18

Thread: Black 8-0

Abdomen: Black mole—can add a bit of olive or brown beaver

Wing: Matched duck quills—dark gray, or gray raffia

Thorax/head: Same as abdomen

Collar hackle: Black, leave a few fibers pointing forward over hook eye when tying off for antennae; hackle also can be palmered over the body and trimmed as desired

Tying Notes: My streamside notebook reveals the size of the natural adult body (abdomen, thorax, head) to range from hook size 17 to 19. The wing extends about one-quarter to one-third of the body length. The color of the abdomen varies between black, olive and brown tones. The black 102Y hook is made to order for the Little Black Caddis.

After dubbing the abdomen, tie in the wing. For the duck quill wing, use thin, matched slips tied back over the abdomen. For the raffia wing, cut a one-inch section of raffia and unfold it (its width will quadruple). Cut a strip of the unfolded raffia parallel to the "crinkles" a little under one-quarter-inch wide. Moisten the strip with your tongue and tie in "tent-style" over the abdomen. Trim to shape. Tie in hackle just ahead of wing, add a bit of dubbing for the thorax, wind hackle and tie off.

Both the duck quill and raffia wings are surprisingly visible. (Raffia winging and tying techniques result from combined tips from the Missouri River Trout Shop in Craig, Montana, and Fly and Field in Glen Ellyn, Illinois.)

Another excellent Black Caddis imitation is tied just like the Cricket (page 87) on a TMC 102Y—size 17 hook, with the wing trimmed to caddis shape.

Fishing Notes:

Little Black Caddis larvae, pupae and adults are very common stomach contents of midwestern trout in April and May. Emergence on spring creeks can be much earlier.

Olive larval patterns, fished deep, will consistently take trout during this period. The adult naturals often appear at mid-day, bringing up good numbers of trout. I prefer fishing the adult imitation whenever possible, usually fished dead drift with 6X or 7X tippet. On occasion, I've run into visibly feeding fish that were selective to the pupa and emerger. A 15-inch brown on the west fork of the Kickapoo refused multiple presentations of the adult but took a pupa on the first cast. The stomach pump revealed nothing but pupae.

Along with Hendricksons (page 54), Baetis (page 47) and Midges (page 40), the Little Black Caddis is an impressive springtime hatch.

American Grannom

This is another dark caddis like the Little Black Caddis only larger. It is very common.

Grannom Emerger

Hook: TMC® 2487—size 14-16

Thread: Black 8-0

Shuck: Poly yarn, gray-thin

Body: Dark olive SLF finesse, mixed with mole

Wing: Snowshoe hare's foot fibers or gray poly yarn

Legs/antennae: Gray partridge fibers

Head: Same as body

Grannom Adult

Hook: TMC 100—size 16

Thread: Olive 8-0

Body: Same as emerger—add bright green egg sac at rear of body
on some flies

Wing: Light gray duck quill, coated with Flexament®
or gray raffia

Collar hackle: Blue dun

Grannom Spent
See Tying Notes.

Tying Notes: Refer to Little Black Caddis (page 74). The duck quill wing is coated at the base with Flexament and tied "tent-style." The collar hackle is wound over a bit of dubbing—add antennae if desired. The Grannom Spent is tied the same as the adult, with raffia or duck-shoulder feathers tied spent and sparse hackle.

Fishing Notes:

The Grannom (Brachycentrus numerous) is found from spring creeks to freestone rivers—look for the "chimney-cased" larvae attached to rocks and branches. This caddis hatches in late April and May, then dwindles. It occurs along with the Little Black Caddis. The adults emerge suddenly and take to the air with wings flashing silver gray. Adults with green egg sacs flutter over the surface in early afternoon, then fall spent in the evening.

The larva ("chimney-cased" peeking caddis, page 32) can be fished anytime. The emerger is fished early and mid-day, followed by the adult in the afternoons and spent patterns in the evening. The Henryville caddis is a useful pattern for matching fluttering adults. (Excellent tying instructions for the Henryville are given in Skip Morris' book *The Art of Tying the Dry Fly.*)

Au Sable River.

Tan Caddis a.k.a. Cinnamon or Spotted Caddis ★

Tan Caddis Adult

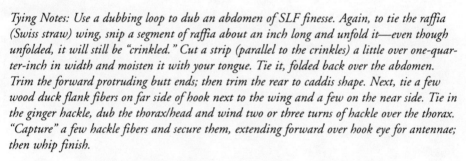

Hook: TMC® 100—size 16; TMC 102Y—size 17

Thread: Brown 8-0

Abdomen: SLF finesse to approximate BCS 55

Wing: Tan raffia (Swiss straw), can use mottled tan-brown hackle tips or folded tan turkey

Legs: Wood duck flank

Thorax: Same as abdomen

Hackle: Ginger

Tying Notes: Use a dubbing loop to dub an abdomen of SLF finesse. Again, to tie the raffia (Swiss straw) wing, snip a segment of raffia about an inch long and unfold it—even though unfolded, it will still be "crinkled." Cut a strip (parallel to the crinkles) a little over one-quarter-inch in width and moisten it with your tongue. Tie it, folded back over the abdomen. Trim the forward protruding butt ends; then trim the rear to caddis shape. Next, tie a few wood duck flank fibers on far side of hook next to the wing and a few on the near side. Tie in the ginger hackle, dub the thorax/head and wind two or three turns of hackle over the thorax. "Capture" a few hackle fibers and secure them, extending forward over hook eye for antennae; then whip finish.

The raffia wing has a very realistic translucence and is nicely visible. Durability is quite good. To test durability, I counted the trout that took one fly and ended up losing the fly on trout number 16—the fly was still in reasonably good condition.

This pattern is effective for different species of Tan Caddis as well. Tie a few in larger sizes and also some size 18 to 22.

For the Tan Caddis Pupa, use the same abdomen and thorax with a ventral wing of gray muskrat and wood duck flank fibers for legs and antennae. The emerger uses a tan poly shuck and snowshoe hare's foot wing, colored tan.

The spent adult simply uses spread "delta" wings.

Fishing Notes:

Tan Caddis emerge on many of our streams from May through September; emergence is usually in the evening. Early in the season, Elk Hair Caddis will work, but as the fish get educated, a more exact imitation is necessary.

The Tan Caddis adult is fished dead drift; an occasional twitch may be needed. To simulate egg-laying adults, the dry pattern is pulled beneath the surface and fished actively—let it swing in the current and twitch retrieve.

Spent adults are fished dead drift. Some of my most frustrating fishing ever occurred with the spent Tan Caddis on Montana's Missouri River. Large fish were visibly feeding with head-tail riseforms in the evening, and selectivity was extreme. The best imitation turned out to be the spent pattern tied with rust colored raffia wings.

Another tough caddis river is Michigan's Muskegon below Croton Dam—a good place to work on your Ph.D. in caddis!

Little Summer Green Caddis a.k.a. Little Sister Sedge

Hook: TMC® 100—size 16-20

Thread: Brown 8-0

Abdomen: SLF finesse, green to approximate BCS 30

Wing: Gray-tan hackle tips to approximate BCS 108

Thorax/head: Olive-brown beaver

Hackle: Brown

Tying Notes: A straightforward tie. A yellow egg sac may be added to some of the adult patterns.

The pupa is tied like the Little Black Caddis (page 72) with a light olive abdomen, brown ventral wings and wood duck flank fibers for legs and antennae.

Fishing Notes:

The dark caddis predominate in spring; the tan and green caddis are more common during the summer. On the stream, I usually try to capture a natural adult for guidance regarding size and color. If the trout are on top, the riseform may be helpful with the decision. Bulging rises may call for a pupa or emerger. Splashy rises indicate the need for a fully hackled adult fished with action. A quiet rise with an air bubble might mean a flush floating adult is needed. If no surface activity is present, a deeply fished pupa or larva is warranted. Spent patterns are generally most useful in the evening, fished dead drift.

The stomach pump on suitably sized fish is very educational but sometimes leads to a dilemma: if the stomach contents differ from your imitation, do you change flies?

Norm Zimmerman fishing the Timber Coulee.

Terrestrials

Fortunately for the fly fisher (unfortunately for the insect), land-based insects fall into the stream, creating splendid fishing situations. I always look forward to choosing imitations from my terrestrial collection, especially hoppers.

Beetles

June Bug

Hook: Mustad® 94840—size 10

Thread: Brown 3-0

Underbody: Brown Australian opossum

Legs: Copper color Krystal Flash® filaments

Overbody: Ethafoam® one-quarter-inch thick

Tying Notes: Wind a base of tying thread along shank. Cut a piece of Ethafoam (packing sheeting) to a width of one-quarter inch and tie-in starting at about one-third shank length behind hook eye and winding backward to hook bend. The foam extends to the rear and will be pulled over later like a wingcase. It should be bound firmly (you'll hear a few pops as the bubbles in the foam break while tying down). The 3-0 thread is used because it doesn't cut into the foam. Next dub the underbody forward. Tie three filaments of Krystal Flash, one-third length behind the eye, perpendicular to the shank, and divide them with thread to give the impression of three legs on each side. Secure the leg tie-in area with head cement or superglue. Pull the foam over and tie down just behind the hook eye. Snip the forward projecting foam, but leave a small extension to mimic the head of the beetle. Reverse fly in vise, arrange legs in proper alignment and secure again with head cement. Trim legs to proper length—the rear legs should be longer. Color the foam with a brown, waterproof marking pen.

Fishing Notes:

The June Bug was designed in response to the pumped stomach contents of a large brown trout taken from Wisconsin's Tomorrow River in May—the fly has not been a disappointment. The natural "hatches" in May and June and the insects are active in the evening but can be found on the water at any time, especially beneath overhanging trees.

The fish seem to remember them long after their emergence period is over. I like to fish the imitation as a searching pattern over holding water beneath streamside willows and basswood, especially if I know of a large brown trout in the vicinity. The fly is very visible, even in rougher water, and it floats very well. Durability is fair—maybe four or five fish per fly. When you see June Bugs around lights at night, it's time to throw a few imitations in your fly box and remember to use them.

BHP Beetle
(Brown-Hackle Peacock)

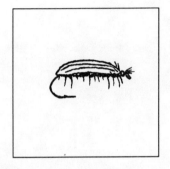

Hook: TMC 100—size 12, 14, 16
Thread: Black 6-0
Underbody: Peacock herl
Hackle: Brown
Overbody: Black Hi-Vis®

Tying Notes: Wrap hook shank with thread, tie in a suitably sized sheaf of Hi-Vis fibers starting about one-third length behind hook eye and wrap back to bend. As in the June Bug, the backward projecting Hi-Vis fibers will form a "wingcase." Tie in brown hackle and peacock herl, reinforce peacock by spiraling it around tying thread and wrap forward. Tie off peacock and palmer hackle forward. Tie off hackle, bring Hi-Vis fibers over the top loosely (if too tight, potential air spaces will close) and tie off. Snip Hi-Vis fibers, leaving a forward extension to mimic the head.

Fishing Notes:

Starting quite early in the season, even in April, trout begin to eat beetles. The BHP Beetle is a "general" imitation that I will use if pump samples reveal that trout have been taking them. Use fly floatant on the body and "head." If visibility is a problem, use an indicator. Sunken terrestrials, especially beetles, crickets and inchworms, can produce awesome results. I never mind when my "dry" terrestrial becomes "wet." The BHP Beetle is a very effective pattern fished dry and downstream over likely holding areas, especially on streams that are low and clear.

Clipped-Hackle Beetle

Hook: TMC® 921—size 18, 20; TMC 101—size 22

Thread: Black 8-0

Hackle: 1 grizzly, 1 brown

Overbody: Black Hi-Vis®

Tying Notes: Tie in Hi-Vis fibers as in BHP Beetle; tie in hackles at rear and palmer forward to just behind hook eye. Trim hackle 360 degrees around hook shank to about half the gap length. Pull Hi-Vis loosely over the top and tie off, leaving a moderate-sized "head" of forward extending fibers.

Fishing Notes:

This imitation was tied in response to summertime trout sipping beneath trees with no apparent surface insects. It took me over an hour to catch a 12-incher and check the stomach sample—small beetles. I could have saved myself some time if I'd carried a small fabric screen (which I now carry) to sample the water below the risers. This imitation is used a few times every summer under similar circumstances. Long tippets, delicate casting and "becoming part of the environment" are important elements for success in this situation.

The Clipped-Hackle Beetle also works well during the summer on small streams, fished along the undercuts with a small amount of weight and an indicator.

Ants

Black Fur Ant

Hook: TMC® 100—size 16, 18, 20

Thread: Black 8-0

Body: Black beaver

Rear legs: Moose

Hackle: Black, wrapped over front segment

Wing: Optional white hackle tips or synthetic

Tying Notes: Dub a ball of fur near bend of hook—be sure to leave a thin "waist" at center of shank. Tie in either moose (one fiber per side, trailing back) or wing (not both). Tie in hackle, dub a smaller ball of fur in front and over-wrap with hackle. Tie both winged and unwinged ants in black and cinnamon. Carry them from late April through late fall.

Fishing Notes:

See Cinnamon Fur Ant, page 84.

Cinnamon Fur Ant

Hook: TMC 100—size 20; TMC 101—size 22, 24

Thread: Light yellow 8-0

Body: Light yellow beaver

Hackle: Cream

Tying Notes: Similar to Black Ant. I usually use light yellow beaver and cream hackle and tint with an orange waterproof felt tip pen.

Fishing Notes:

Vern Lunde of Lunde's Fly Fishing Chalet in Mt. Horeb, Wisconsin, relates that he was fishing a stream in South Dakota, casting to sizable and finicky risers that wouldn't move an inch out of their feeding lanes. He wasn't doing quite as well as he'd liked, so he switched to an ant. The first cast was a few feet off target, but he noticed an immediate submarine-like wake approaching his ant, which was then inhaled by the first trout in the pod—sometimes trout do that with ants.

I landed an 18-inch brown on the south branch of the Oconto that had the highest number of individual food items I have ever found in one fish—thousands of small Cinnamon Ants. Trout love to sip ants, and stomach samplings reveal ants from mid-April well into the fall. Consider ants when you see bankside sippers. Winged patterns are definitely easier to see.

Fall Flying Ant

Hook: TMC® 100—size 14, 16

Thread: Brown 8-0

Abdomen: Yellow SLF, mixed with yellow Australian opossum

Thorax: Brown Australian opossum

Underwing: Twinkle organza

Overwing: Elk hair

Hackle: Brown, clipped top and bottom

Tying Notes: Tie a prominent yellow abdomen and just a bit of brown thorax. Tie in underwing; then hackle and add a bit more thorax dubbing. Wind hackle over thorax, trim and tie in sparse elk hair overwing.

Fishing Notes:

I was fishing the tailwater section of the Oconto River below Stiles in late October, and the small Blue-Winged Olives were coming off heavily with the attendant rising trout—some of them quite large (holdover migrants from Lake Michigan). It took a frustrating 20 minutes to realize the trout weren't on the Olives. Close examination of the surface revealed flying ants with large yellow abdomens, clear wings and a brown thorax. Fortunately, I was still carrying my caddis box, and it contained a reasonable imitation of the ants. I caught fish the rest of the afternoon, including one 20-inch brown. The Fall Flying Ant was "tied and tried" for this situation.

I carry a good supply each fall for fishing Lake Michigan tributaries.

Inchworm

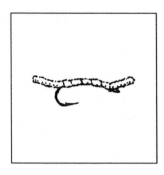

Hook: TMC® 2312—size 14

Thread: Light yellow 6-0

Body: Insect green or fluorescent yellow Vernille®

Tying Notes: Tied like a San Juan Worm (page 17) only shorter and less tapered. Can be tied with extended deer hair body or SLF (green) dubbed and trimmed.

Fishing Notes:

The naturals make their appearance in June—you'll see them precariously hanging by their threads from branches over the stream, unaware of the danger lurking from below. Hopefully, the trout are unaware of the danger of an imitation, fished dead drift, on or beneath the surface in wooded areas of the stream. The chenille version will float on the first cast; then it becomes a sub-surface imitation, but the fluorescent colors are still very visible. Try it with added weight and an indicator.

Cricket ★

Hook: TMC® 100—size 16

Thread: Black 8-0

Abdomen: Dark brown Australian opossum—can add black or olive SLF

Wing: Dark turkey flat from wild bird

Legs/head/antennae: Black deer hair

Tying Notes: This is a pattern, with minor variations, from Tom Wendelburg, a master fly fisherman and fly designer from Middleton, Wisconsin. Tom introduced his Cricket to me on a guided trip several summers ago, and I've carried it ever since, modified slightly for ease of tying.

Dub a plump abdomen and tie in wing, coated with Flexament®, flat over the back, trimmed to a rounded shape. Tie in deer hair, fibers extending forward over hook eye and long enough to represent legs when pulled back. (Wind the tying thread right up to the eye when tying in the deer hair, then back the length of the head.) Trim deer hair butts. Pull back one-half of deer hair and secure on far side of hook, repeat with remaining fibers on near side. Splay fibers away from body and "touch" with head cement. Pull a few deer hair fibers over the bullet-head and tie down to represent antennae. Tie off immediately behind hook eye.

Fishing Notes:

This is an important summertime fly on our midwestern meadow streams from mid-June through fall—it has a longer period of usefulness than the Hopper. The Cricket produced two brown trout—one 21 inches and one 22 inches in a period of one and one-half hours on the west fork of the Kickapoo one afternoon in late June (see Colorplate 14). Both fish were sighted feeding near the surface, and each took the Cricket presented about one foot to the near side of the fish and slightly behind their heads. I saw each fish turn and looked right down their white mouths as they took the fly—both were hooked in the upper palate. (I think they "taste" the Crickets by pushing them into their palate with their tongue.) Experiencing times like this, when large trout are exposed and on the feed, then connecting with them, is one of fly-fishing's great pleasures.

The Cricket, in size 17, can also double as a Black Caddis as I found out one evening on the Bighorn. Vince Marinaro's point about the importance of antennae is a good one—the Bighorn fish definitely preferred the imitations with intact antennae.

Hackle-Wing Hopper ★

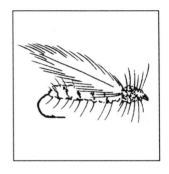

Hook: TMC® 2312—size 10, 14

Thread: Orange 6-0

Abdomen: Yellow SLF mixed with yellow Antron®

Body hackle: Brown hackle

Wing: Tan-ginger barred hackle feathers from Chinese or Indian neck

Thorax: Rust-brown SLF mixed with purple Antron

Thorax hackle: Brown

Tying Notes: This Hopper is easy to tie—it is basically a delta-wing stimulator. Start the tying thread and take to rear of hook—leave a tag end and dub abdomen loosely to about one-third shank length behind eye. Tie in body hackle, wind it backward and secure with forward wraps of tag end. Pick out body fibers a bit. Next take two hackle feathers for the wings and "cup" together, lay them over the shank, tips pointing back, and tie in both feathers together, shiny side up. The tips should extend a bit beyond the hook bend. Secure the butts firmly and snip butt ends. Splay the feathers delta-wing style, one to each side with a wrap of thread. Tie in thorax hackle, dub thorax/head, wind hackle forward and tie off.

Be sure to crimp the barb on these flies because the trout often take them deep into their mouths.

Fishing Notes:

I'll generally use Crickets as my main terrestrial pattern in June and July, then start with Hoppers in late July. Conditions at this time are far different from when we started with the Gray Leech (page 11) in January/February. Water temperatures on some streams can approach the 80's—concentrating the trout in riffles and below small cool water tributaries. It is best not to stress fish in this situation. Go to a cool running spring creek or a stream without a temperature problem.

By July, the trout have become very well-educated, and streams are low and clear—conditions that demand the best of your fly-fishing skill. Several factors work in our favor. For example, trout metabolize their food more rapidly and need to feed more often, and trout love terrestrials, particularly Hoppers.

Hoppers start to become active from mid-morning into afternoon, and the fish are aware of this. Trout definitely look for them. A nice feature about Hopper time is that it is also Trico time. Fish Tricos early in the morning; then switch to Hoppers. Later you can fish Tan Caddis (page 77) or Pseudocloeon (page 47).

To fish the Hopper on meadow streams, go slow and low—camouflage yourself. Keep your rod tip down and don't flash the flyline over the fish. Use the finest tippet you can get away with. Don't overlook thin water if there is even a hint of cover, such as overhanging grass. In the woods, fish shaded areas beneath low-hanging branches. I took a 21-inch brown (pictured on the back cover and below) from beneath an overhanging willow with a downstream cast on the Hackle-Wing Hopper; the take was very gentle. Fish a downstream dry fly by using the "bounce feed" (see Swisher casting videos, information page 98).

On heavily fished streams, try different casting angles. If everyone is casting to a holding area from the same angle, try a new approach. The Hackle-Wing Hopper is capable of moving good fish, either up from the depths or laterally, away from snags. Fish the snags with a "plopped" Hopper a foot or two away from the "fly catching" snag. Hoppers should be twitched now and then—a "plop" and a "twitch" can be deadly. The Hackle-Wing Hopper, like the BHP Beetle, is very effective fished downstream to likely holding water.

The Hackle-Wing Hopper is good at night during hot weather—it's not very visible, but you'll know when to strike. The pattern floats a bit low, and visibility isn't as good as a clipped deer hair or foam imitation. Durability is good; with a crimped barb, you should get 15-20 trout per fly. This is an all-star fly!

Special Flies and Attractors

Presented in this section are three famous flies of Midwest origin: the Adams, the Pass Lake Dry and the Hornberg. Also presented is one "all world" fly, the Royal Wulff.

Adams ★

Hook: TMC® 100—size 12 through 20; TMC 101—size 22

Thread: Gray 6-0, 8-0

Tail: Grizzly hackle fibers

Body: Gray muskrat

Wing: Grizzly hackle tips

Hackle: One grizzly, one brown

Tying Notes: The Adams, for good reason, is one of the most famous flies in the world. It has a Michigan origin. I wonder how many trout have been taken on this fly and its many variations. Tying instructions and photos are given in Kaufmann's Tying Dry Flies. My favorite variation is the Parachute Adams, tied with a post of white calf body hair. An Adams Wulff, tied with a moose hair tail and split white calf hair wings, is useful in larger sizes.

Fishing Notes:

In a full day's fishing, I'll usually tie on some form of Adams sometime during the day. One of the most beautiful brown trout I've seen was caught by my friend, Norm Zimmerman; it was 24 inches long and took a size 20 Adams on the Castle Rock.

A Parachute Adams (or a "Grizzly Parachute" tied without the brown hackle) is nearly universally acceptable to trout, either fished alone or as an indicator dry fly with a small nymph trailing behind.

Either the traditional or Parachute Adams is a good choice if you feel like fishing a dry fly without surface activity. Use the Adams Wulff on "heavy" water.

The Adams is the universal answer to the question, "If you had to pick just one dry fly, which would it be?"

Pass Lake Dry

Hook: TMC® 100—size 14-20

Thread: Black 6-0, 8-0

Tail: Mallard flank fibers

Body: Black chenille or peacock herl

Wing: White calf body hair tied behind hackle "trude style"

Hackle: Brown

Tying Notes: This is a straightforward pattern to tie. Tie in tail and chenille (very fine chenille is best), wind chenille forward and tie off. Add the white calf hair-wing tied "trude style"; then tie in and wind hackle.

Fishing Notes:

This down-wing attractor is excellent. (Also see the White Calf Hair Down-Wing Attractor, page 69.) Both the chenille and peacock bodies "draw" into the film, and after a few casts, the pattern becomes a "damp" fly that is highly visible. The Pass Lake Dry is useful in brushy areas and is easily fished downstream with action. It is a particularly good brook trout fly. Like the Adams, it is useful on all kinds of water.

Hornberg

Hook: TMC® 5212—size 10, 14

Thread: Black 6-0, 8-0

Body: Silver tinsel

Underwing: Few fibers of yellow deer hair

Overwing: Mallard flank feathers and slips of barred black and white wood duck flank feather

Hackle: Grizzly

Tying Notes: First wrap the tinsel body; then add a few yellow deer hair fibers on top about one-quarter shank length behind eye. Strip flue and fibers from mallard flank feather down to proper size and tie one feather on each side of hook (concave side in). Add wood duck slips next to mallard, tie in hackle, wrap and tie off.

Fishing Notes:

The versatile Hornberg is named after its designer, Frank Hornberg of Portage County, Wisconsin. I particularly like to fish this pattern downstream, under branches and logs, usually dead-drifting down-current. I let it swing, then either skitter it back on the surface or pull it under and twitch retrieve.

The Hornberg produces consistent action. Trout hooked downstream are more prone to "long distance releases" (LDR), and these fish are usually "very large." I've lost a few fish like this.

Royal Wulff

Hook: TMC® 100—size 10, 14 18

Thread: Black 6-0, 8-0

Tail: Moose

Body: Peacock—fluorescent red floss—peacock

Wing: White calf body hair, divided

Hackle: Brown

Tying Notes: Royal Wulffs are not difficult to tie, especially with a rotary vise. Tie a few large and medium Wulffs and a lot of small ones. Again, see Kaufmann's Tying Dry Flies *book.*

Fishing Notes:

Like the Adams, the Royal Wulff is a universally fished fly. It combines visibility, durability, floatability and outstanding trout appeal. It is the classic attractor. The Au Sable Wulff and the Black Wulff are excellent variations.

Hatch Chart

HATCH CHART

Numbers of Naturals — Small | Medium | Large | Variable (V)

PATTERN/INSECT		JAN	FEB	MAR	APR	MAY	JUNE	JULY	AUG	SEPT	OCT	NOV	DEC
MIDGES		▓	▓	▓	▓	▓	▓	▓	▓	▓	▓	V	▓
MAYFLIES													
	Hendrickson					▓	▓						
	Sulphurs					▓	▓						
Carpet Fly & H.W. Adams	"Stenonema"					▓	▓	▓				V	
	Brown Drake						▓						
	Isonychia Sp.											V	
	Gray Drake						▓						
	Light Cahill						▓	▓	▓				
	Hexagenia Limbata							▓	▓				
	Tricorythodes								▓	▓	▓		
	White Mayfly								▓	▓			
Blue-Winged Olive Patterns	Baetis Sp.			▓	▓	▓	▓	▓	▓	▓	▓		
	Paraleptophlebia Sp.				▓	▓							
	Ephemerella Sp.					▓	▓						
	Pseudocloeon Sp.								▓	▓	▓		
LITTLE YELLOW STONEFLY							▓	▓					
YELLOW CRANEFLY							▓	▓	▓				
CADDISFLIES													
	Little Black Caddis			▓	▓	▓							
	American Grannom				▓	▓							
	Tan Caddis					▓	▓	▓					
	Little Summer Green Caddis						▓	▓	▓				
TERRESTRIALS													
	June Bug						▓	▓					
	BHP Beetle					▓	▓	▓	▓				
	Clipped-Hackle Beetle					▓	▓	▓	▓	▓			
	Black Fur Ant					▓	▓	▓	▓	▓	▓	V	
	Cinnamon Fur Ant					▓	▓	▓	▓	▓	▓	V	
	Fall Flying Ant						▓	▓	▓	▓	▓		V
	Inchworm						▓						
	Cricket					▓	▓	▓	▓	▓	▓		
	Hackle-Wing Hopper							▓	▓	▓	▓		

Approximate emergence periods for "central" areas. Subject to variability due to weather conditions and location. Midge and Ant emergence are often locally very heavy.

GUIDES TO INSECT IDENTIFICATION

Caddisflies, by Gary LaFontaine. New York: Nick Lyons Books, 1981.

Hatches II, by Al Caucci and Bob Nastase. Piscataway, New Jersey: Winchester Press, 1986.

Mayflies, The Angler and the Trout, by Fred L. Arbona, Jr. New York: Lyons and Burford Publishers, 1989.

Matching the Hatch, by Ernest Schwiebert, Jr. The Macmillan Company, 1955. Reprinted by Stoeger Publishers, South Hakensack, New Jersey.

Naturals, A Guide to Food Organisms of Trout, by Gary A. Borger. Harrisburg, Pennsylvania: Stackpole Books, 1980.

Trout Stream Insects, An Orvis Streamside Guide, by Dick Pobst. New York: Lyons and Burford Publishers, 1990.

TROUT STREAM INFORMATION

DeLorme Atlas and Gazetteer. Available for Michigan, Minnesota and Wisconsin, by DeLorme Mapping. Freeport, Maine.

Fishing Regulation Booklets available from respective state Department of Natural Resources.

Iowa Trout Fishing Guide, by Iowa Department of Natural Resources (maps of Iowa's trout streams). Des Moines, Iowa.

Iowa Trout Streams, by Jene Hughes. Des Moines, Iowa: Second Avenue Bait House Publisher.

Michigan Trout Streams, A Fly Angler's Guide, by Linsenman and Nevala. Woodstock, Vermont: Back Country Publishers, 1993.

Trout Anglers Guides (seven booklets for seven important Michigan trout streams). Available from Challenge Chapter of Trout Unlimited, PO Box 63, Bloomfield Hills, Michigan.

Trout Fishing in Southeast Minnesota, by John van Vliet. Highwater Press, 1992.

Trout Streams of Southeast Minnesota, by Minnesota Department of Natural Resources (maps of southeast Minnesota trout streams). St. Paul, Minnesota.

Twelve Classic Trout Streams in Michigan, by Gerth Hendrickson. Ann Arbor, Michigan: University of Michigan Press.

Wisconsin and Minnesota Trout Streams, by Jim Humphrey and Bill Shogren. Woodstock, Vermont: Back Country Publishers, 1995.

Wisconsin Trout Streams, Publication Number 6-3600 (80), by Wisconsin Department of Natural Resources (important resource book for all Wisconsin trout water). Madison, Wisconsin.

FLY TYING

The Art of Fly Tying, by John van Vliet. Cy DeCosse Inc., 1994.

The Art of Tying the Dry Fly, by Skip Morris. Portland, Oregon: Frank Amato Publications, 1993.

Designing Trout Flies, by Gary A. Borger. Wausau, Wisconsin: Tomorrow River Press, 1991.

The Dry Fly, New Angles, by Gary LaFontaine. Helena, Montana: Greycliffe Press, 1990.

The Emergence Schedule Book. A Guide to Matching the Insect Hatches of Michigan Trout Streams. Available from Challenge Chapter of Trout Unlimited, PO Box 63, Bloomfield Hills, Michigan.

The Fly Tier's Companion, by Mike Dawes. South Hackensack, New Jersey: Stoeger, 1989.

The Fly Tier's Manual, by Mike Dawes. South Hackensack, New Jersey: Stoeger, 1989.

The Fly Tyer's Nymph Manual, by Randall Kaufmann. Portland, Oregon: Western Fisherman Press, 1986.

Hatches of the Muskegon River, by Carl Richards. A monograph. (Deals with Caddis imitations.)

A Modern Dry Fly Code, by Vince Marinaro. A. P. Putnam's Sons, 1950; Crown Publishers, Inc., 1970.

Production Fly Tying, by A. K. Best. Boulder, Colorado: Pruette Publishing, 1989.

The Soft Hackle Fly, by Sylvester Nemes. Stackpole Publishing. 1993 reprint of 1975 edition.

Tying Dry Flies, by Randall Kaufmann. Portland, Oregon: Fisherman Press, 1991.

Tying Nymphs, by Randall Kaufmann. Portland, Oregon: Western Fisherman Press, 1994.

What the Trout Said, by Datus Proper. Knopf, New York, 1982. Reprinted by Nick Lyons Books, 1989.

USEFUL STREAMSIDE INFORMATION BOOKS

Borger Color System, by Gary A. Borger. Wausau, Wisconsin: Borger Enterprises, Inc., 1986.

Fly Fishing Strategy, by Doug Swisher and Carl Richards. New York: Crown Publishers, 1975.

Nymph Fishing for Larger Trout, by Charles E. Brooks. New York: Reprinted by Lyons and Burford, 1988.

Nymphing, A Basic Book, by Gary A. Borger. Harrisburg, Pennsylvania: Stackpole Books, 1979.

Presentation, by Gary A. Borger. Wausau, Wisconsin: Tomorrow River Press, 1995.

Selective Trout, by Doug Swisher and Carl Richards. New York: Crown Publishers, 1971.

Stalking Trout, by Les Hill and Graeme Marshall. Auckland, New Zealand: Halcyon Press and SeTo Publishing, 1985.

The Trout and the Fly, by Brian Clarke and John Goddard. New York: Lyons and Burford, 1988.

Trout Stream Therapy, by Robert L. Hunt. Madison, Wisconsin: University of Wisconsin Press, 1993.

FUN READING

Fishing a Highland Stream, by John Inglis Hall. Putnam & Company, Ltd., 1960.

A River Runs Through It, by Norman Maclean. University of Chicago Press, 1976.

Trout Madness, by Robert Traver. New York: St. Martins Press, 1960.

CASTING VIDEO REFERENCES

Advanced Fly Casting, by Doug Swisher

Basic Fly Casting, by Doug Swisher

The Essence of Fly Casting, by Mel Krieger

The Essence of Fly Casting II, Advanced Fly Casting, by Mel Krieger

Video Fly Casting with Lefty Kreh, by Gary Borger Enterprises

AUDIOTAPE

River Rap Series—The Wolf River, with Gary La Fontaine and Wayne Anderson. Greycliffe Press, Helena, Montana.

Index

W

Y

Z